Motorcycle
modifying
The definitive guide

Motorcycle
modifying
The definitive guide

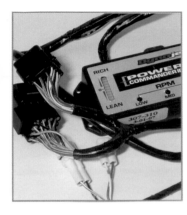
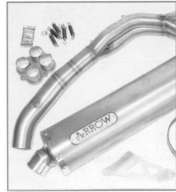

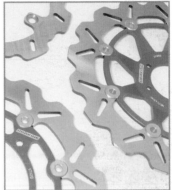

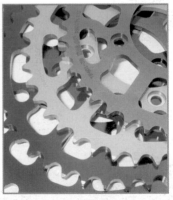

by Pete Gill

ISBN 1 84425 272 8

Library of Congress Control Number 2005927834

Printed by J H Haynes & Co Ltd,
Sparkford, Yeovil, Somerset BA22 7JJ, England

Tel: 01963 442030 Fax: 01963 440001
Int. tel: +44 1963 442030 Fax: +44 1963 440001
E-mail: sales@haynes.co.uk
Web site: www.haynes.co.uk

Haynes North America, Inc
861 Lawrence Drive, Newbury Park, California
91320, USA

Editions Haynes
4, Rue de l'Abreuvoir
92415 COURBEVOIE CEDEX, France

Haynes Publishing Nordiska AB
Box 1504, 751 45 UPPSALA, Sweden

It wasn't my idea officer!

1 Advice on safety procedures and precautions is contained throughout this manual, and more specifically on pages 10 and 11. You are stongly recommended to note these comments, and to pay close attention to any instructions that may be given by the parts supplier.

2 J H Haynes recommends that motorcycle modifying should only be undertaken by individuals with experience of motorcycle mechanics; if you are unsure as to how to go about the modification, advice should be sought from a competent and experienced individual. Any queries regarding modification should be addressed to the product manufacturer concerned, and not to J H Haynes, nor the motorcycle manufacturer.

3 The instructions in this manual are followed at the risk of the reader who remains fully and solely responsible for the safety, roadworthiness and legality of his/her motorcycle. Thus J H Haynes are giving only non-specific advice in this respect.

4 When modifying a motorcycle it is important to bear in mind the legal responsibilities placed on the owners, riders and modifiers of motorcycles, including, but not limited to the Road Traffic Act 1988. IN PARTICULAR, IT IS AN OFFENCE TO RIDE ON A PUBLIC ROAD A MOTORCYCLE WHICH IS NOT INSURED OR WHICH DOES NOT COMPLY WITH THE CONSTRUCTION AND USE REGULATIONS, OR WHICH IS DANGEROUS AND MAY CAUSE INJURY TO ANY PERSON, OR WHICH DOES NOT HOLD A CURRENT MOT CERTIFICATE (IF REQUIRED) OR DISPLAY A VALID TAX DISC.

5 The safety of any alteration and its compliance with construction and use of regulations should be checked before a modified motorcycle is sold as it may be an offence to sell a motorcycle which is not roadworthy.

6 Any advice provided is correct to the best of our knowledge at the time of publication, but the reader should pay particular attention to any changes of specification to the motorcycles, or parts, which can occur without notice.

7 Alterations to motorcycles should be disclosed to insurers and licensing authorities, and legal advice taken from the police, vehicle testing centres, or appropriate regulatory bodies.

8 The motorcycles featured in this book represent some of the most popular models for modifying and readers should not assume that the motorcycle manufacturers have given their approval to the modifications.

9 Neither J H Haynes nor the manufacturers give any warranty as to the safety of a motorcycle after alterations, such as those contained in this book, have been made. J H Haynes will not accept liability for any economic loss, damage to property or death and personal injury arising from use of this manual other than in respect of injury or death resulting directly from J H Haynes' negligence.

Contents

Introduction 8

Safety 10

Security equipment 12

Security at home 15

Security away from home 15

Security

Clear lenses 16

Indicators 18

LEDs 20

Headlight bulbs 21

Headlight covers 22

Mirrors 23

Lighting & mirrors

Dial kits 25

Digital gear indicator 25

Engine management display 30

Visual Display

Bars and controls

Clip-ons 71

Bar grips 72

Rear sets 73

Chain and Sprockets

Front sprocket 80

Rear sprocket 81

Chain 82

Gear ratio 86

Chain care 86

Chainguards 87

Wheels and tyres

Tyres 88

Wheels 91

Spark plugs	33
Clutches	34
Exhausts	35
Filters	40
Fuel and ignition control	42

Performance

04

Suspension adjustment	47
Rear shock upgrades	52
Front fork upgrades	54
Swingarms	55
Steering dampers	56

Suspension and steering

05

Pads	61
Brake fluid	62
Discs	62
Braided hoses	66
Radial front brake master cylinder	68

Brakes

06

10

Bodywork

Screens	94
Tank pads	97
Fuel caps	98
Undertrays	100
Carbon fibre	105
Body panels	109
Decals	114
Bolt kits and bling	116

11

Trackdays

Preparation	119
Programme	120
Crash protectors	123
Toe guards	127
Engine casings	128

12

Reference

Tools	131
Tech terms	134
Index	140
Thanks to:	142
Haynes Bike Manual listing	144

Introduction

The motorcycle aftermarket is massive, with a vast array of components available for today's superbikes. Some owners limit changes to a screen, undertray and end can, whereas others pursue the more exotic world of carbon fibre race components and serious engine mods. The aim is the same, to improve on the standard bike and give it an individual identity – the difference is in the financial investment.

The aim of this book is to show how to fit many of the popular aftermarket components, and in the Haynes tradition, to pass on the hints and tips gained from doing the work ourselves. Fitting instructions are supplied with most aftermarket parts; a few are comprehensive and supported by further information on their maker's websites, but others may either assume a high level of knowledge on the part of the owner or be woefully inadequate.

Regardless of our wish to promote our core product service and repair manuals, we strongly advise that you have access to a specific workshop manual for your machine. The fitting of most aftermarket components will require a certain amount of dismantling, and the procedures

Before ...

for doing so are not always immediately obvious. Furthermore, the workshop manual will provide torque setting data and in the case of fitting electrical components access to a full wiring diagram will prove invaluable.

A year 2000 Honda CBR929RR-Y forms the subject for most photographic procedures in the book and its transformation from standard to modified form is shown in the pictures below.

When choosing modified parts, take time to read product reviews in the motorcycle press and consult the leading suppliers; most have websites and catalogues and are happy to discuss fitments. It's a good idea to retain all the original equipment parts you replace because future owners may prefer to revert some components back to standard form. Modified bikes, whilst tastefully prepared in most cases, are likely to attract a higher value if the owner is able to provide the standard parts.

Although many new bikes are modified within days of leaving the showroom, this could invalidate the warranty provided by the manufacturer. There's no hard and fast rule here, as it depends on the nature of any problems which might occur within the warranty period, but it is a point to consider.

Always inform your insurance company when you modify the machine. This applies particularly if the modification increases the power of the bike and alters its performance. If you have had a one-off paint job done on the bike, you may find that the insurance company will not insure the bike due to the high cost of replicating a damaged panel. You will usually find that they are more concerned about the greater risk of theft of a modified machine than the fitting of performance increasing components.

Bear in mind the information in chapter 1 concerning security; many aftermarket components are of a high value and easily unbolted unless care is taken to secure them well.

... After

Safety

Professional mechanics are trained in safe working procedures. However enthusiastic you may be about getting on with the job at hand, take the time to ensure that your safety is not put at risk. A moment's lack of attention can result in an accident, as can failure to observe simple precautions.

There will always be new ways of having accidents, and the following is not a comprehensive list of all dangers; it is intended rather to make you aware of the risks and to encourage a safe approach to all work you carry out on your bike.

Asbestos

● Certain friction, insulating, sealing and other products - such as brake pads, clutch linings, gaskets, etc. - contain asbestos. Extreme care must be taken to avoid inhalation of dust from such products since it is hazardous to health. If in doubt, assume that they do contain asbestos.

Fire

● Remember at all times that petrol is highly flammable. Never smoke or have any kind of naked flame around, when working on the vehicle. But the risk does not end there - a spark caused by an electrical short-circuit, by two metal surfaces contacting each other, by careless use of tools, or even by static electricity built up in your body under certain conditions, can ignite petrol vapour, which in a confined space is highly explosive. Never use petrol as a cleaning solvent. Use an approved safety solvent.

● Always disconnect the battery earth terminal before working on any part of the fuel or electrical system, and never risk spilling fuel on to a hot engine or exhaust.

● It is recommended that a fire extinguisher of a type suitable for fuel and electrical fires is kept handy in the garage or workplace at all times. Never try to extinguish a fuel or electrical fire with water.

Fumes

● Certain fumes are highly toxic and can quickly cause unconsciousness and even death if inhaled to any extent. Petrol vapour comes into this category, as do the vapours from certain solvents such as trichloro-ethylene. Any draining or pouring of such volatile fluids should be done in a well ventilated area.

● When using cleaning fluids and solvents, read the instructions carefully. Never use materials from unmarked containers - they may give off poisonous vapours.

● Never run the engine of a motor vehicle in an enclosed space such as a garage. Exhaust fumes contain carbon monoxide which is extremely poisonous; if you need to run the engine, always do so in the open air or at least have the rear of the vehicle outside the workplace.

The battery

● Never cause a spark, or allow a naked light near the vehicle's battery. It will normally be giving off a certain amount of hydrogen gas, which is highly explosive.

● Always disconnect the battery ground (earth) terminal before working on the fuel or electrical systems (except where noted).

● On conventional fillable batteries, loosen the filler plugs or cover when charging the battery from an external source. Do not charge at an excessive rate or the battery may burst.

● Take care when topping up (fillable batteries), cleaning or carrying the battery. The acid electrolyte, evenwhen diluted, is very corrosive and should not be allowed to contact the eyes or skin. Always wear rubber gloves and goggles or a face shield. If you ever need to prepare electrolyte yourself, always add the acid slowly to the water; never add the water to the acid.

Electricity

● When using an electric power tool, inspection light etc., always ensure that the appliance is correctly connected to its plug and that, where necessary, it is properly grounded (earthed). Do not use such appliances in damp conditions and, again, beware of creating a spark or applying excessive heat in the vicinity of fuel or fuel vapour. Also ensure that the appliances meet national safety standards.

● A severe electric shock can result from touching certain parts of the electrical system, such as the spark plug wires (HT leads), when the engine is running or being cranked, particularly if components are damp or the insulation is defective. Where an electronic ignition system is used, the secondary (HT) voltage is much higher and could prove fatal.

Remember...

✗ **Don't** start the engine without first ascertaining that the transmission is in neutral.

✗ **Don't** suddenly remove the pressure cap from a hot cooling system - cover it with a cloth and release the pressure gradually first, or you may get scalded by escaping coolant.

✗ **Don't** attempt to drain oil until you are sure it has cooled sufficiently to avoid scalding you.

✗ **Don't** grasp any part of the engine or exhaust system without first ascertaining that it is cool enough not to burn you.

✗ **Don't** allow brake fluid or antifreeze to contact the machine's paintwork or plastic components.

✗ **Don't** siphon toxic liquids such as fuel, hydraulic fluid or antifreeze by mouth, or allow them to remain on your skin.

✗ **Don't** inhale dust - it may be injurious to health (see Asbestos heading).

✗ **Don't** allow any spilled oil or grease to remain on the floor - wipe it up right away, before someone slips on it.

✗ **Don't** use ill-fitting spanners or other tools which may slip and cause injury.

✗ **Don't** lift a heavy component which may be beyond your capability - get assistance.

✗ **Don't** rush to finish a job or take unverified short cuts.

✗ **Don't** allow children or animals in or around an unattended vehicle.

✗ **Don't** inflate a tyre above the recommended pressure. Apart from overstressing the carcass, in extreme cases the tyre may blow off forcibly.

✔ **Do** ensure that the machine is supported securely at all times. This is especially important when the machine is blocked up to aid wheel or fork removal.

✔ **Do** take care when attempting to loosen a stubborn nut or bolt. It is generally better to pull on a spanner, rather than push, so that if you slip, you fall away from the machine rather than onto it.

✔ **Do** wear eye protection when using power tools such as drill, sander, bench grinder etc.

✔ **Do** use a barrier cream on your hands prior to undertaking dirty jobs - it will protect your skin from infection as well as making the dirt easier to remove afterwards; but make sure your hands aren't left slippery. Note that long-term contact with used engine oil can be a health hazard.

✔ **Do** keep loose clothing (cuffs, ties etc. and long hair) well out of the way of moving mechanical parts.

✔ **Do** remove rings, wristwatch etc., before working on the vehicle - especially the electrical system.

✔ **Do** keep your work area tidy - it is only too easy to fall over articles left lying around.

✔ **Do** exercise caution when compressing springs for removal or installation. Ensure that the tension is applied and released in a controlled manner, using suitable tools which preclude the possibility of the spring escaping violently.

✔ **Do** ensure that any lifting tackle used has a safe working load rating adequate for the job.

✔ **Do** get someone to check periodically that all is well, when working alone on the vehicle.

✔ **Do** carry out work in a logical sequence and check that everything is correctly assembled and tightened afterwards.

✔ **Do** remember that your vehicle's safety affects that of yourself and others. If in doubt on any point, get professional advice.

● If in spite of following these precautions, you are unfortunate enough to injure yourself, seek medical attention as soon as possible.

Security

After spending so much money on fitting aftermarket parts, the last thing you want is your bike stolen. There are many security devices on the market ranging from disc locks to alarms and immobilisers. While fitting a security device does not guarantee your bike won't be stolen, it will serve as a good deterrent.

In less time than it takes to read this introduction, a thief could steal your bike. Returning only to find your bike has gone is one of the worst feelings in the world. There is nothing quite so depressing as having your pride and joy stolen by someone out to make easy money at your expense. Even if the bike is insured against theft, once you've got over the initial shock, you will have the inconvenience of dealing with the police and your insurance company.

Bike thefts fall into two categories, those stolen 'to order' and those taken by opportunists. The bike thief stealing to order will be on the look out for a specific make and model and will go to extraordinary lengths to obtain that bike – they may dismiss modified bikes for this reason. The opportunist thief on the other hand will look for easy targets, such as bikes which can be stolen with the minimum of effort and risk.

Whilst it is never going to be possible to make your machine 100% secure, it is estimated that around half of all stolen bikes are taken by opportunist thieves. Remember that the opportunist thief is always on the look out for the easy option, if there are two similar bikes parked side-by-side, they will target the one with the lowest level of security. By taking a few precautions, you can reduce the chances of it being your bike.

Security equipment

There are many specialised bike security devices available and the following text summarises their applications and their good and bad points.

Once you have decided on the type of security equipment which best suits your needs, we recommended that you read one of the many equipment tests regularly carried out by the bike press. These tests compare the products from all the major manufacturers and give impartial ratings on their effectiveness, value-for-money and ease of use. This should help to ensure you purchase the best value product available.

No one item of security equipment can provide complete protection. It is highly recommended that two or more of the items described below are combined to increase the security of your bike (a lock and chain combined with an alarm system is just about the ideal combination). Remember that the more security measures fitted to the bike, the less likely it is to be stolen.

Lock and chains

A lock and chain is the most common type of security used, and can be used in a number of different ways. Ensure the lock and chain you buy is of good quality and long enough to shackle your bike to a solid object. If parking up with a friend's bike, it can be useful to lock the two bikes together.

Never carry the lock and chain

around your body when riding – in the event of an accident it would cause an injury.

Pros: Very flexible to use; can be used to secure the bike to almost any immovable object. On some locks and chains, the lock can be used on its own as a disc lock.

Cons: Can be very heavy and awkward to carry on the bike, although some types will be supplied with a carry bag which can be strapped to the pillion seat.

Heavy-duty chains and locks are an excellent security measure. Whenever the bike is parked, use the lock and chain to secure the machine to a solid, immovable object such as a solid post or railings. This will prevent the machine from being ridden away or being lifted into the back of a van. If the bike is parked in the same spot regularly (e.g. at work), then the lock and chain can be left fastened around the post or secure railings to save carrying it home.

When fitting the chain, always ensure it is routed around the bike frame or swingarm. Never merely pass the chain around one of the wheel rims; it is not unheard of for a thief to unbolt the wheel and lift the rest of the machine into a van, leaving you with just the wheel! Try to avoid having excess chain free, thus making it difficult to use cutting tools, and try to keep the chain and lock off the ground to prevent thieves attacking it with a cold chisel. Also try to position the lock so that its lock barrel is facing downwards; this will make it harder for the thief to attack the lock mechanism.

U-locks

U-locks can be used to secure the bike to a solid object (or D-locks as they are somethimes known), ensure you purchase one which is long enough.

Pros: Highly effective deterrent which can be used to secure the bike to a solid post or railings. Most U-locks come with a carrier which allows the lock to be stowed on the bike.
Cons: Not as flexible to use as a lock and chain.

These are solid locks which are similar in use to a lock and chain. U-locks are lighter than a lock and chain but not so flexible to use. The length and shape of the lock shackle seriously limits the type of objects to which the bike can be secured.

Disc locks

Pros: Small and light and very easy to carry; most can be stored underneath the seat.
Cons: Does not prevent the bike being lifted into a van. Can be very embarrassing if you forget to remove the lock before attempting to ride off!

Always fit the disc lock up against the brake caliper or fork leg. In this way, should you forget to remove it, the bike will not be able to move straight away. If this precaution isn't observed, you could damage the disc, mudguard, caliper or even fall off the bike if you attempt to ride off with the disc lock on! Disc lock warning cables are available, which fasten to the bars or levers to remind you there is a disc lock fitted.

Disc locks are designed to be attached to the front brake disc. The lock passes through one of the holes in the disc and prevents the wheel rotating by jamming against the fork/brake caliper. Some disc locks are equipped with an alarm siren which sounds if the disc lock is moved; this not only acts as a theft deterrent but also as a handy reminder if you try to move the bike with the lock still fitted.

Combining the disc lock with a loop of cable which can be looped around a solid post or railings provides an additional measure of security.

Brake lever lock

This lock is similar to the disc lock in size and is easy to carry on the bike. It fits around the right-hand handlebar and brake lever, holding the front brake on.

Security bolts

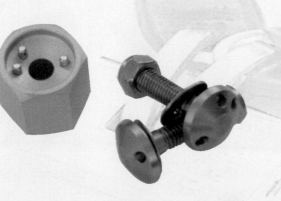

These bolts require a special key to release them. When expensive aftermarket components are fitted to your bike it gives an added level of security. Security bolts are commonly used on exhaust cans and tax disc holders.

Alarms and immobilisers

Pros: Once the system is installed on the bike it is completely hassle-free to use. If the alarm/immobiliser system is 'Thatcham or Sold Secure-approved', insurance companies may give you a discount on your annual premium. Thatcham is the appointed body responsible for setting the security standard for motorbikes.
Cons: Can be expensive to buy and some systems are complex to install. No system will prevent the bike from being lifted into a van and taken away.

Electronic alarms and immobilisers are available to suit a variety of budgets. There are three different types of system available: those which are purely anti-theft alarms, others which are purely immobilisers, and the more expensive systems which are combined alarm/immobilisers.

An alarm system is designed to emit an audible warning if the bike is being tampered with, thus drawing attention to the bike and causing the thief to flee the scene for fear of being discovered.

An immobiliser prevents the bike being started and ridden away by disabling its electrical systems (an immobiliser is usually connected into the starter motor circuit and ignition circuit).

When purchasing an alarm/immobiliser system, always remember to check the cost of installing the system unless you are able to install it yourself. If the bike is not used regularly, another consideration to bear in mind is the current drain of the system. All alarm/immobiliser systems are powered by the bike's battery; purchasing a system with a very low current drain could prevent the battery losing its charge whilst the bike is not being used.

Security marking kits

Datatag – Smartwater - Alphadot – Ultraviolet pen – Security stickers
Pros: Very cheap and effective deterrent. Many insurance companies will give you a discount on your insurance premium if a recognised security marking kit is used on your bike.
Cons: Does not prevent the bike being stolen by joyriders.

There are many different types of security marking kits available. The idea of the kit is to mark as many individual parts of the bike as possible with a unique security number. A form will be included with the kit for you to register your personal details and those of the bike with the kit manufacturer. This register is made available to the police to help them trace the rightful owner of any bike or bike components which they recover should all other forms of identification, such as engine and frame numbers, have been removed from the bike. Always apply the warning stickers provided with the kit to deter thieves.

Ground anchors, wheel clamps and security posts

Pros: An excellent form of security which will deter all but the most determined of thieves.

Cons: Awkward to install and can be expensive.

Whilst the bike is at home, it is a good idea to attach it securely to the floor or a solid wall, even if it is kept in a securely locked garage. Various types of ground anchors, security posts and wheel clamps are available for this purpose. These security devices are either bolted to a solid concrete or brick structure or can be cemented into the ground.

Security at home

A high percentage of bike thefts are from the owner's home. Here are some things to consider whenever your bike is at home:

- Where possible, always keep the bike in a securely locked garage. Never rely solely on the standard lock on the garage door, these are usually hopelessly inadequate. Fit an additional locking mechanism to the door and consider having the garage alarmed. A security light, activated by a movement sensor, is also a good investment. You could also consider placing a "baby monitor" inside the garage.
- Always secure the bike to the ground or a wall, even if it is inside a securely locked garage.
- Do not regularly leave the bike outside your home, try to keep it out of sight wherever possible. If a garage is not available, always fit a bike cover over the bike to disguise its true identity. A thief is unlikely to go to the trouble of removing the cover just to find out what type of bike is underneath.
- It is not uncommon for thieves to follow a motorcyclist home to find out where the bike is kept. They will then return at a later date and steal your bike under the cover of darkness. Note that thieves have been known to pose as potential buyers to find out where bikes are kept and then return later to steal them.

Security away from home

As well as fitting security equipment to your bike here are a few general rules to follow whenever you park in a public place.

- Park in a busy, public place.
- Use public car parks which incorporate security features, such as CCTV.
- At night, park in a well-lit area, preferably directly underneath a street light.
- Engage the steering lock.
- Secure the bike to a solid, immovable object such as a post or railings with an additional lock. If this is not possible, secure the bike to a friend's bike whom you are travelling with. Note that some public parking places provide security loops for bikes.
- Never leave luggage attached to the bike, take it with you at all times.

Lighting and Mirrors

Clear tail light lens

Check that the tail light unit has a red inner lens – this enables the standard clear bulbs to be used. If a red inner lens is not fitted, bulbs which illuminate red when operated will be required. Note that on models where the tail light also illuminates the licence plate, separate provision must be made to ensure the licence plate is illuminated by a white light – see the Undertray section in the Bodywork chapter for details.

Clear tail light lenses are easy to fit and simply bolt in place of the standard red lens without any modification.

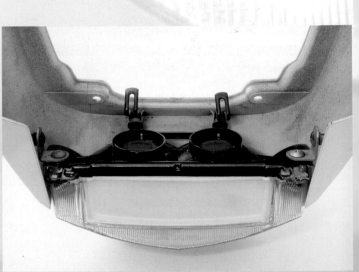

On this model it was necessary to remove the tail unit to access the tail light lens mountings.

Clear indicator lenses

Note that unless the clear lenses have an inner orange lens, bulbs which illuminate orange when operated will be required.

1 Slacken and remove the retaining screw from the indicator.

2 Withdraw the indicator lens from the surround. Turn the bulb holder to release it.

4 Insert the bulb holder and turn it to lock it in place in the clear lens unit.

3 Remove the standard clear bulb from the bulb holder and fit the orange bulb.

5 Refit the clear lens unit back into the indicator surround and tighten the retaining screw.

Indicators

Aftermarket indicators are available in various styles, sizes, colours and materials. Lenses are available in standard orange colour, clear, iridium and smoked options. Most are universal fitting, the most common being flush mount, cats eye, diamond and arrow head. Aftermarket indicators also come in mini and micro form.

Fitting rear mini indicators

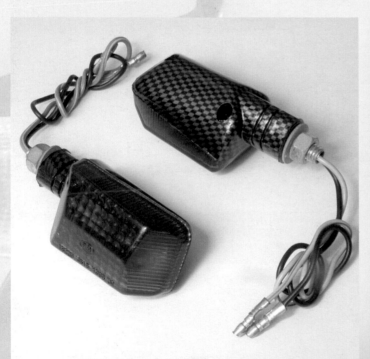

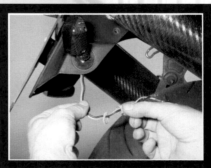

2 Fit the new mini indicator, using the original mounting washer from the standard indicator.

3 With the indicator in position, fit the washer and nut over the wiring. Feed the wires back up under the seat and reconnect them. You may need to fit new wiring connectors to match those fitted to the bike.

1 Remove the original indicators from the bike. Disconnect the wiring (the connectors are usually under the seat), then undo the retaining bolt/nut and withdraw the indicator.

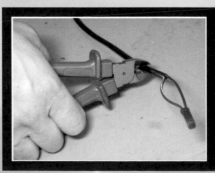

4 Rather than cutting the bike's wiring loom, it is preferable to cut the wiring connector off the standard indicator, leaving enough wire to connect to the new mini indicator wiring.

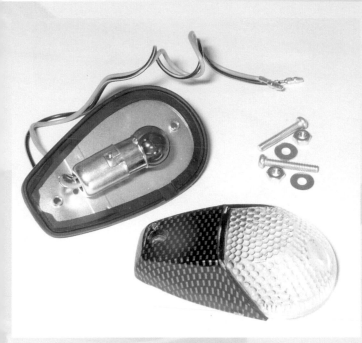

Fitting front flush mounted indicators

Before purchasing flush ,pimted indicators, check the size of the opening in the panel where the indicator stalk comes through. Measure across the diameter of the opening to make sure the type of indicator you purchase covers the hole completely.

Note that many fitments require holes to be drilled in the fairing panel to mount the indicator.

Indicator mounting plates are available for certain models. They attach to the fairing and enable the fitting of aftermarket indicators.

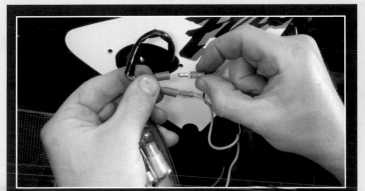

4 Connect the wiring connectors, then fasten the wiring securely behind the fairing panel. Rather than cutting the bike's wiring loom, it is preferable to cut the wiring connector off the standard indicator, leaving enough wire to connect to the new indicator's wiring.

1 Undo the retaining bolt/nut and disconnect the wiring to remove the standard indicator from the bike.

2 Hold the flush fitting indicator against the fairing panel to check its alignment and mark the mounting bolt holes.

5 With the lens cover fitted, align the mounting bolts with the holes in the fairing panel.

3 Drill two holes in the panel.

6 Fit the nuts and washers to the mounting bolts and tighten them securely.

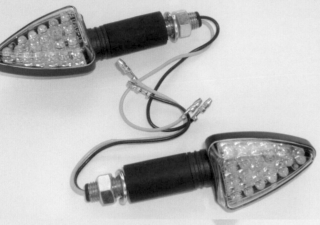

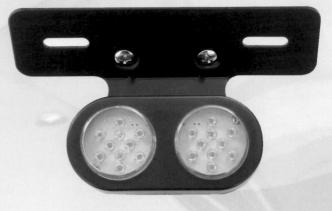

Light emitting diodes (LEDs)

Indicator and stop/tail light units are available which incorporate a series of LED's instead of standard bulbs. Tail light units have built in resistors to enable a weaker light for the tail light and a brighter light when the brake is operated. Some LED indicator units require a resistor in the wiring circuit to control their flash rate.

LED type bulbs are available with a bayonet fitment and simply replace the original bulb. The actual number of LEDs varies between bulb types. LED bulbs have a longer life than standard bulbs, so not only do they look cool but you will rarely have to replace them.

Remove the standard stop and tail bulbs and simply fit the LED bulbs.

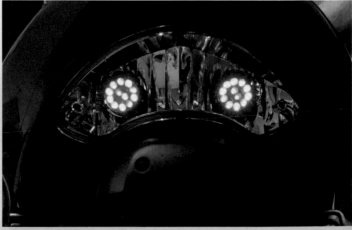

These tail light LEDs illuminate red. Where the tail light also illuminates the licence plate, you'll need to make separate provision for a licence plate light.

Headlight bulbs

Blue Vision bulbs give off a blue bright light (4000°K (Kelvin)) which is longer lasting.

Vision Plus bulbs give the highest possible light output for road use, with up to 50% more light and a 10 to 20 metre longer range than standard bulbs.

Weather vision bulbs give off a yellow light for better visibility in bad weather conditions. More commonly used for fog lights.

Blue bulbs are also available for side lights.

WARNING

Do not be tempted to fit the highest wattage headlight bulbs available – if the bulb wattage is too high it may be illegal. Also note that high wattage bulbs produce more heat which could melt plastic lenses, and the increased wattage could overload the wiring or switch unit.

Rainbow strobes

Rainbow strobes are bulb covers which filter the standard white light to create a rainbow effect. The filters do not effect the light's visual effectiveness and work particularly well in rain and fog. They are usually supplied in pairs to use with H4 halogen bulbs

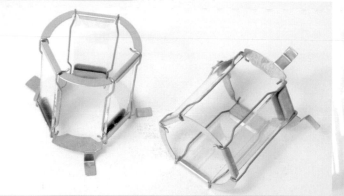

2 Insert the rainbow strobe bulb cover into the headlight unit; there are three locating pegs to fit the headlight bulb aperture.

3 With the rainbow strobe bulb cover in place, the headlight bulb can then be fitted.

1 The H4 halogen bulb fits inside the rainbow strobe.

4 The bulb covers are made up of a glass prism to reflect the colours around the headlight and create a rainbow of primary colours.

Headlight covers

Headlight covers are available in the same range of colours as screens. Aside from their aesthetic value, a headlight cover will protect the headlight from damage by stone chips. Note that in the UK, only clear (or possibly yellow) covers are considered legal for road use.

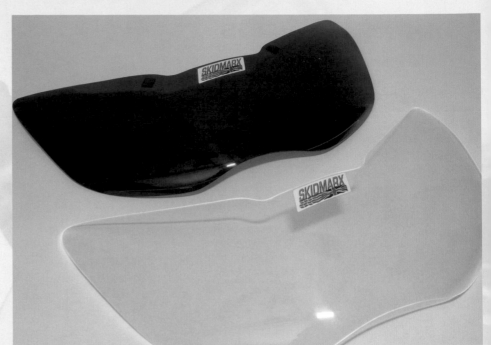

Fitting a headight cover

1 Use methylated spirits to wipe any dirt and bugs from the headlight. Dry the headlight with a soft cloth.

2 Remove the backing tape from half of the fixing pads and stick them to the inside of the headlight cover.

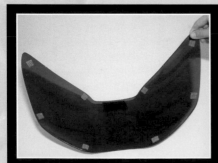

3 Make sure the fixing pads are spaced out equally around the cover edges.

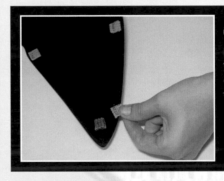

4 Engage the other half of the fixing pads with those you've stuck to the cover, then remove their backing tape.

5 Carefully align the cover with the headlamp and press it firmly into place. For best results do not use the bike for the next 12 hours to allow time for the fixing pads to bond securely.

6 After the fixing pads have bonded securely, the cover can then be removed and refitted as required. Pull at the mounting points to release.

Mirrors

Aftermarket mirrors are available in various colours and materials, including carbon fibre. Many are more streamlined than those fitted as original equipment, but check first that their position and viewing area is sufficient.

Although most mirrors are universal fitting, check the mounting point measurements to ensure a perfect and secure fixing. The mirrors are supplied as a swivel or fixed assembly, with either a flat or convex mirror glass.

If you find it difficult to see past your elbows when riding, there is also the option of bar end mirrors for that wide angle view.

A more streamlined look can be achieved by the fitting of integral indicators and mirrors.

Alloy blanking plates can be fitted if the mirrors are removed, such as for track use. Plates are available plain or engraved.

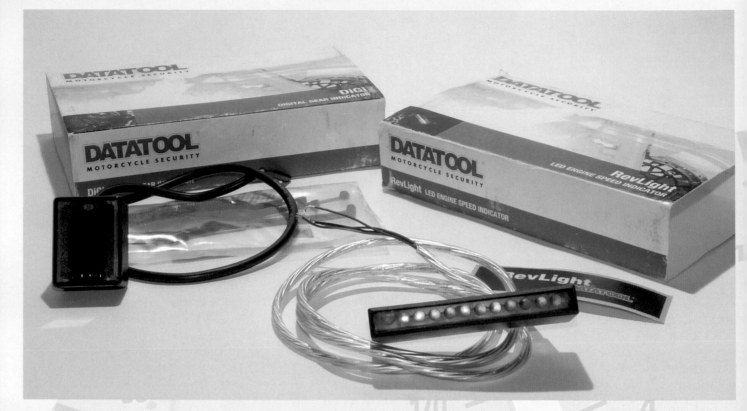

Visual display

Rider display accessories range from a simple temperature gauge to a full digital dash display system.

Although the fitting of electrical components may appear daunting, the components are usually supplied with fitting instructions and often there's a contact number or website for technical queries. Check that all components are in the fitting kit and read through the instructions thoroughly. It would also be wise to obtain a specific wiring diagram for your bike so that the electrical connections can be fully understood. If after reading the instructions you have any doubt about the fitment, consult an expert before cutting any wires.

WARNING

For safety reasons you should disconnect the battery before disconnecting or cutting any wiring.

Dial kits

Dial kits are a great way to change the appearance of analogue instruments. White dials with blue digits or yellow dials with black digits are common types, but other colours are available. Some dial kit manufacturers are even able to create a dial kit to your own design, incorporating logos.

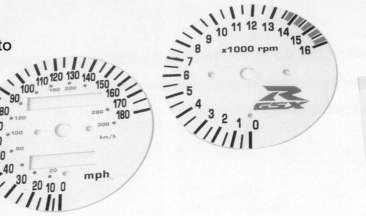

Most kits are of the overlay type, which have an adhesive backing and simply stick onto the original gauge. It will be necessary to remove the instrument cluster and partially strip the instruments to access to the dials. Depending on your technical ability, a workshop manual for your specific bike may be required.

Higher spec dial kits of the "electro luminescent" type show white dials during daylight, but change colour at night, with the digits illuminated in **RED** and **BLUE**. They require an electrical source and are usually wired into the headlight loom via a simple two wire connection. The dials consist of an overlay which simply sticks over the original black dials; there is no need to remove the needle as the overlay is designed to slip over it. A dimmer control switch is also supplied.

For bikes with KPH clocks, dial kits are an ideal solution to converting the speedometer to show MPH and considerably cheaper than buying new instruments. Note that the speedometer may need to be re-calibrated to display the correct values.

Digital gear indicator

The digital gear indicator is suitable for most modern bikes fitted with an electronic speedometer and tachometer. It can, however, be adapted for use on bikes with a cable-driven speedo by fitting an upgrade kit.

Several kits are available, each offering alternative colour display options and other features such as auto-dimming for night use. Fitting instructions are provided with the kit or can be downloaded from the manufacturer's website (see the "Thanks to" section at the end of this book).

Short wiring looms are available for certain models to enable easy installation (called a "plug and go" loom), whereas on others it will be necessary to splice into the bike's wiring loom to make the connections. Check if a loom is available for your model bike, because this will save you a lot of time on fitting. Where it is necessary to splice in the wiring connectors note that the preferred option is to solder them in place.

Wire connectors will need to be fitted to the wiring supplied in the fitting kit. The type of connectors to be fitted will vary depending on model of bike being worked on.

Fitting the digital gear indicator

This procedures illustrates the fitting of an Acumen DG8 gear indicator. The wiring connections are spliced into the bike's wiring loom in this case. After fitting the unit and making the wiring connections, refer to the Programming procedure.

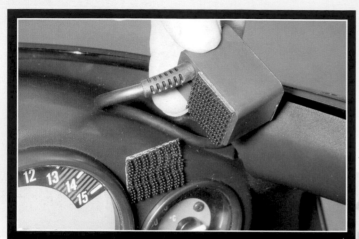

1 Decide where the digital gear indicator unit will be mounted. The unit is held in place with Velcro, so once positioned it can then be removed to carry on with the installation.

2 Remove any fairing trim panels, screen and instrument surrounds as necessary to gain access to the wiring loom at the rear of the instruments.

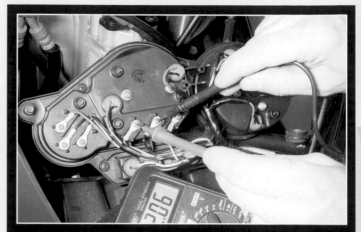

3 Use a voltmeter (set to 0 to 20 dc volts range) to check the wiring at the rear of the instrument panel. With the ignition on, a positive (+) wire and negative (-) wire were located at the rear of the tachometer.

4 In this case the kit's red wire (positive), black wire (negative), and brown wire (tacho. feed) have been connected to the rear of the tachometer. The green wire was then spliced into the wire from the neutral light (which goes to the neutral light switch). Where an electronic speedo is fitted the orange wire from the kit would be spliced into the wire from the back of the speedo which goes to the speed sensor. On this bike, which has a cable-driven speedo, the orange wire is connected to the blue wire of the upgrade kit.

Wire connections

Red wire – connect to a wire that becomes positive when the ignition is switched on (NOT lights or indicators).

Green wire – connect to the wire which runs from the neutral light bulb and earths through the neutral light switch.

Orange wire – connect to the wire which runs from the speed sensor to the electronic speedo. On bikes with a cable-driven speedo, connect to the upgrade kit.

Brown wire – connect to the tachometer feed wire.

Black wire – connect to an earth (negative) wire in the wiring loom (do not earth to the fairing frame).

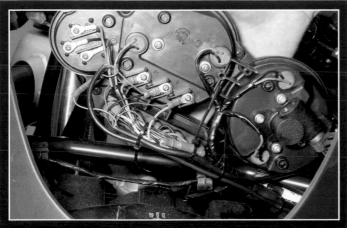

5 Make sure all the wiring is secured neatly using the cable-ties provided in the fitting kit. When all the wiring has been connected securely, the fairing trim panels and any other components that have been removed can now be refitted.

6 When attaching the digital gear indicator unit to the instrument panel, allow some slack in the cable. It must be possible to access the hole in the rear of the display unit for programming.

Programming the digital gear indicator

The engine will need to be run throughout this process, so make sure you are in a well ventilated area. Support the bike on a rear paddock stand, on level ground, so that the rear wheel is well clear of the surface. The engine will be run at speeds up to 4000 rpm through all the gears, so it is vitally important to ensure that nothing will foul the rear wheel as it is spinning. If the speedometer is operated by the front wheel (as in a cable-driven arrangement), this procedure will need to be carried out while the bike is moving along on the road – see overleaf.

Step 1 – programming the number of gears

1   With the engine running and neutral selected, check the display shows 'n' for neutral.
2   Insert the programming key in the back of the unit and hold it in for approx. 10 seconds, until an 'L' (Learn) appears on the display, then remove the programming key.
3   With the 'L' indicated on the display, insert the programming key and press once for every gear the bike has. Every press will indicate 1, 2, 3, 4, 5, 6. Stop at the top gear for your bike.
4   Remove the programming key from the display unit and wait 5 seconds, until 'n' for neutral appears on the display. Leave the engine running and proceed to the next section.

Step 2 – programming the gear ratios

Note: If the engine is switched off at anytime throughout this procedure, then you will need to start the step 2 procedure from the beginning.

1   Select first gear, let the clutch out and run the engine between 2000 and 4000 rpm, until number 1 flashes on the display. Three bars will then appear on the display followed by number 2 – at this point select neutral. This is only required selecting between first and second gear change.

2   Select second gear, run the engine between 2000 and 4000 rpm, until number 2 flashes on the display. Three bars will then appear on the display followed by number 3.
3   Select third gear, run the engine between 2000 and 4000 rpm, until number 3 flashes on the display. Three bars will then appear on the display followed by number 4.
4   Select fourth gear, run the engine between 2000 and 4000 rpm, until number 4 flashes on the display. Three bars will then appear on the display followed by number 5.
5   Select fifth gear, run the engine between 2000 and 4000 rpm, until number 5 flashes on the display. Three bars will then appear on the display followed by number 6.
6   Where applicable, select sixth gear, run the engine between 2000 and 4000 rpm, until number 6 flashes on the display.
7   You can now change down the gears back into neutral and turn the engine off. As you are going down through the gears the gear indicator should display the relevant gear positions.

Installation trouble-shooting

Fault	Fix
'n' does not appear on the display	Check the green wire has been connected to the correct side of the neutral bulb. Also check the neutral light bulb and the fuse have not blown.
Lower segments on the display constantly recycle.	Check the connections at the speedometer and tachometer are correct. Programming procedure may need to be repeated.

If any other faults are shown, then it will be best to go through the fitting procedure again and check all the wiring connections

Speedo cable upgrade kit for Digital Gear Indicator

The speed sensor kit can be operated by the front or the rear wheel, and mounted on the front fork leg or the rear swingarm respectively. The sensor picks up wheel speed from the magnets set in the brake disc, and relays this information in the form of electronic pulses to the digital gear indicator unit.

If the sensor is fitted to the front wheel, programming of the gear indicator must be carried out whilst riding the bike. Access to a rolling road is preferable, otherwise conduct this on a stretch of private road, not the public highway; the procedure should be complete within one mile. Follow the step 2 procedure on the previous page for programming the gear ratios, but instead of having the bike on a paddock stand, you will need to ride it.

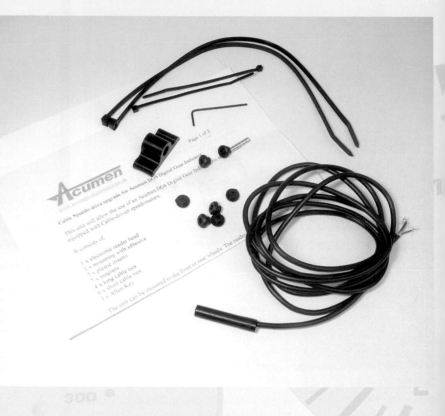

Wire connections

Red wire – connect to a wire that becomes positive when the ignition is switched on (NOT lights or indicators).
Blue wire – connect to the orange wire of the digital gear indicator.
Green wire – connect to an earth (negative) wire in the wiring loom (do not earth to the fairing frame).

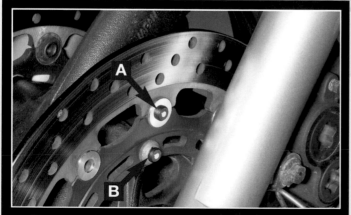

1 The magnets can either be fitted to the head of the Allen bolts which mount the disc to the wheel (A) or to the rivets which hold the outer and inner disc rotors together (B).

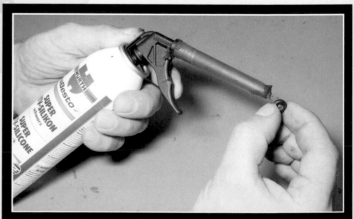

2 Use a silicone sealant to hold the magnets in place. The 7 magnets supplied in the kit do not have to be equally spaced, e.g. if there are 10 rivets around the disc, you can fit all 7 magnets if required.

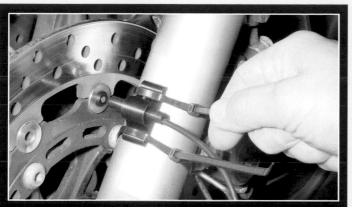

3 Align the sensor with one of the magnets and cable-tie its mounting block to the fork leg. The mounting block is fixed with a high bond pad on its rear surface so ensure the fork leg is clean and free from any grease before mounting the block.

6 Use the cable ties supplied to secure the sensor wire along the length of the speedo cable and run the wiring up to the rear of the instruments.

4 Slide the sensor in the mounting block and position it so that the gap between its tip and the magnet is no more than 20mm.

7 On the bike shown the red wire (positive) and the green wire (negative) were connected to the rear of the tachometer, together with the wiring from the digital gear indicator unit . . .

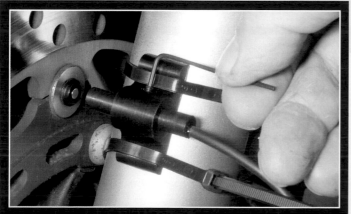

5 Using an Allen key, tighten the grub screw in the mounting block to prevent the sensor from moving out of position. Do not over-tighten the grub screw.

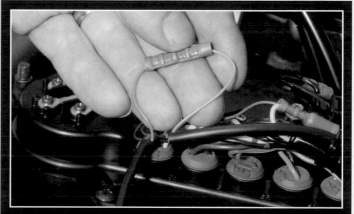

8 . . . and the blue wire was connected to the orange wire from the digital gear indicator at the back of the speedometer.

Engine management display

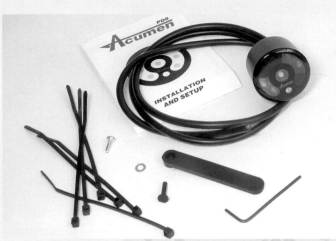

The engine management display unit can be set up to give an indication of engine speed or as a form of rev light warning or shift light, depending on how it is programmed. The unit can be programmed repeatedly, so if you are doing a track day and you want the lights to illuminate at the optimum gear change point, then all you need to do is re-programme it. The unit also has an auto dim function for riding at night.

The unit can be programmed to display the following functions:

Tachometer – lights will show a sequential display.
Gearchange light – lights will come on at the optimum rpm.
Road speed reminder – lights set to come on at speed limit required.
Ideal fuel consumption – lights will come on at the best rpm to change gear.

Fitting the engine management display

This procedures illustrates the fitting of an Acumen PD8 engine management display. After fitting the unit and making the wiring connections, refer to the Programming procedure.

Wire connections

Red wire – connect to a wire that becomes positive when the ignition is switched on (NOT lights or indicators).
Black wire – connect to an earth (negative) wire in the wiring loom (do not earth to the fairing frame).
Brown wire – connect to the tachometer feed wire.

2 The unit can be mounted with Velcro, the plastic mounting arm which comes in the kit, or you could make up an aluminium mounting bracket as shown. If making up a bracket, check that the mounting screw doesn't go in too far and damage the display unit.

4 Where required, undo the retaining screws and remove the fairing trim panels, screen and instrument surround to gain access to the wiring loom.

1 Decide where to mount the display unit. In this example the display unit will illuminate sequentially through the rev range and receive signals from the bike's tachometer.

3 The unit will need to be programmed, so access to the rear of the unit must be possible.

5 On this bike, access to the wiring loom was possible by removing the left-hand front indicator panel.

Programming the engine management display

The engine will need to be run throughout this process, so make sure you are in a well ventilated area. It is recommended that the engine is at normal operating temperature for this procedure and the idle speed is set to its correct rpm. Read through the programming procedure beforehand to determine how you are going to set up the unit – there is very little time between the programming steps to make decisions!

6 With the ignition on, locate a positive (+) wire, a negative (-) wire and the tachometer feed wiring. Use a voltmeter (set to the 0 to 20 dc volts range) to check the wiring at the block connector. A wiring diagram will be useful to identify the wire colours.

7 With the wires located, splice the three wires from the engine management display into the wiring loom. Make sure all the wiring is secured neatly using the cable-ties provided in the fitting kit. When the wiring has been connected securely, the fairing trim panels can be refitted.

Step 1 – programming idle speed and 3000 rpm

A   With the engine running, insert the programming key in the back of the unit and hold it in for approx. 10 seconds, the LEDs will scroll for approximately 1.5 seconds then stop at LED 1 – remove the programming key.
B   With LED 1 flashing and the engine at the correct idle speed, insert the programming key and press once. The LEDs will scroll and stop at LED 3 – remove the programming key.
C   With LED 3 flashing increase the engine speed to 3000 rpm, then insert the programming key and press once. The LEDs will scroll and stop – LED 1 and LED 2 will stay on. Remove the programming key. *With the idle speed and 3000 rpm set, you now have just 30 seconds to input your specific use programme.*

Step 2 – programming the display for specific use

This programme is provided as an example and has a starting point for the LEDs of 2300 rpm, an end point of 8500 rpm and a shift/gear change setting of 4200 rpm – modify as required to suit your needs.

Starting point for LEDs to illuminate (example 2300 rpm)

1   LED 1 and LED 2 will stay on: LED 1 shows programming the start of the sequence – LED 2 shows programming in thousands. Press the programming key twice (for 2000 rpm), LED 2 will go out with each press. Wait 3 seconds.
2   LED 1 and LED 6 will stay on: LED 6 shows programming in hundreds. Press the programming key three times (for 300 rpm), LED 6 will go out with each press. The LEDs will scroll.

Ending point for LEDs to illuminate (example for 8500 rpm)

3   LED 7 and LED 2 will stay on: LED 7 shows programming the end of the sequence – LED 2 shows programming in thousands. Press the programming key 8 times (for 8000 rpm), LED 2 will go out with each press. Wait 3 seconds.
4   LED 7 and LED 6 will stay on: LED 6 shows programming in hundreds. Press the programming key five times (for 500 rpm), LED 6 will go out with each press. The LEDs will scroll.

Centre LEDs to illuminate (example for 4200 rpm)

5   Centre LED and LED 2 will stay on: LED 2 shows programming in thousands.
Press the programming key 4 times (for 4000 rpm), LED 2 will go out with each press. Wait 3 seconds.
6   Centre LED and LED 6 will stay on: LED 6 shows programming in hundreds.
Press the programming key twice (for 200 rpm), LED 6 will go out with each press. The LEDs will scroll and stop.

The engine management display can be re-programmed as many times as required. Press the programming key on the back of the display in for 2 to 4 seconds – the LEDs will scroll and then stop. Now follow the Step 2 procedures from 1 to 6, entering the required rpm settings.

To make the LEDs operate anti-clockwise instead of clockwise, set the highest rpm setting first "Starting point for LEDs to illuminate" and then set the lowest rpm setting after "Ending point for LEDs to illuminate".

There is an option to customise the display's four segments - refer to the fitting instructions for details.

Performance

This chapter deals with typical modifications which will increase the engine's performance and which are well within the scope of doing in the home workshop. Serious engine mods such as gas flowing, porting, skimming, turbo charging and nitrous kits are well outside the scope of this book.

Have the bike dyno'd before making any engine improvements. This will be useful benchmark information when assessing the effects of the modified components at a later date. Even if you decide to keep the engine in standard form, the dyno test will show whether it is running efficiently.

Before fitting engine performance parts make sure the bike is in good mechanical order, otherwise much of the benefits will be lost. Most mods will require a certain amount of dismantling, so ensure you have a workshop manual to hand and take a bit of time to find out where the components are located, such as the ECU, so that you can assess whether it's a job for you or someone more experienced.

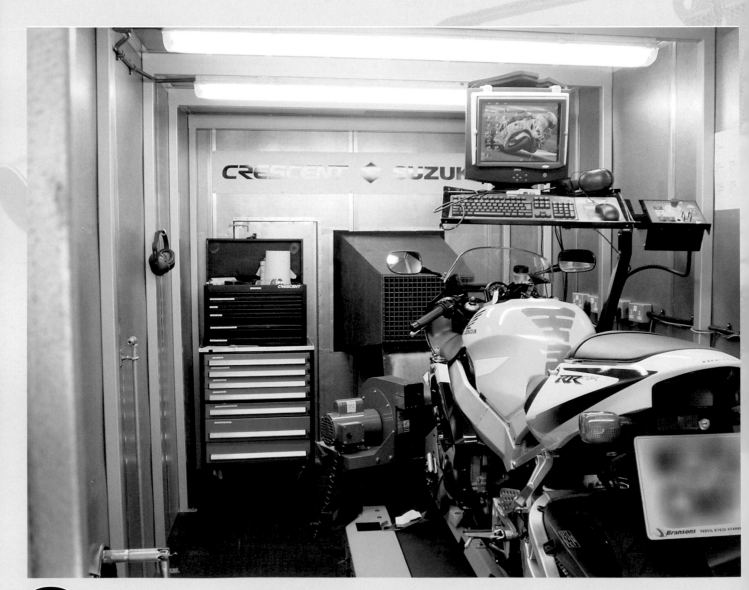

Spark plugs

High performance engines require plugs which can cope with extreme heat yet still give excellent performance. Aside from their thread size, reach and electrode arrangement, spark plugs differ in terms of the materials used. The more expensive plugs often use Nickel, Tungsten or Platinum electrodes for improved performance, longer life and resistance to fouling.

The Iridium plug has a much higher melting point and is six times stronger than platinum electrode plugs. Its centre electrode can be made much smaller than conventional plug types; the narrower the centre electrode, the lower the voltage required to jump the gap to the earth electrode. The benefits of the Iridium plug are improved ignition performance, better fuel consumption, increased power and improved throttle response.

Iridium plugs are fitted as original equipment by certain motorcycle manufacturers and a service life of around 20,000 miles can be expected.

Plug leads

For bikes which use conventional plug leads, the fitting of high performance silicone ignition leads is recommended when upgrading the spark plugs. Their benefit is less electrical resistance and thus an improved spark.

Taylor motorcycle leads are produced in different lengths and colours. Matching suppressor caps are available in long or short, angled or straight styles.

Ignition coils

Aftermarket ignition coils are available for bikes which use conventional coil and spark plug lead systems. These coils can produce in excess of 30000 volts and are designed to give maximum performance.

Check the coil primary resistance value specified by the bike manufacturer. Dyna ignition coils are produced in a range of five different types having primary resistances from 0.7 ohms up to 5.0 ohms – make sure the correct value coil is fitted.

Performance clutch

Do not overlook the clutch when carrying out engine improvements, for many of these gains can be lost if the clutch is not transferring engine power efficiently to the transmission. The original clutch, with plates and springs in good condition, may well prove adequate, but you might need to consider a clutch upgrade if engine power output has been increased considerably or if demanded by your riding style!

Clutch plates

The **"K" series** performance clutch plate is the most common fitment for road and race bikes. The Kevlar friction material used works exceptionally well at high temperatures and lasts longer than standard clutch plate material. Kevlar is very durable and enables a smooth and positive clutch action. K series plates are compatible with standard steel plates, springs and regular engine oil – no other changes are required.

The **"CF" series** performance clutch plates have the same benefits as Kevlar plates, but use carbon fibre friction material. These plates are intended mainly for racing.

Clutch springs

Uprated clutch spring sets are usually supplied in the performance clutch plate kit, but are also available to purchase separately.

Clutch spring conversion kits are available for bikes which use a diaphragm spring clutch, such as the

Yamaha YZF-R1. The multi-coil spring fitment is the more common fitment and considered to give a more positive, controlled clutch action.

Slipper clutch

Slipper clutches are in common use on race bikes and fitted as original

equipment on a few road bikes. Slipper clutches are also available as aftermarket parts.

The slipper clutch overcomes the problem of the rear wheel trying to lock (chatter) under heavy braking, by automatically disengaging the clutch to smooth power delivery. The rider is then able to focus on getting around the corner as fast as possible without having to slip the clutch manually. As soon as engine power is re-applied, the clutch then re-engages instantly to restore the drive.

Radial clutch master cylinder

On bikes fitted with an hydraulic clutch, improved lever action can be gained by the fitting of a radial master cylinder. The radial master cylinder differs from the original unit in that the piston is perpendicular to the clutch lever, rather than parallel to the lever. The span of the lever is adjustable to suit the rider's requirements.

The main sizes produced by Brembo are 19 x 18 (recommended for Aprilia, Honda, Kawasaki, Suzuki and Triumph models) and 16 x 18 (for Ducati models). The size specification 19 x 18, indicates a 19mm bore diameter and a distance of 18mm from the fulcrum and point of support to the piston rod.

Exhausts

The standard exhaust can is usually the first thing to be uprated after purchasing a bike.

Most race cans will give a power increase of around 4 bhp over standard cans and full systems will give an increase of around 8 bhp. Race cans, however, are not road-legal in the UK. Without any other modifications, however, a race can/exhaust will not necessarily improve performance despite sounding louder. The full benefit is only usually gained by first running a dyno test to determine the engine's fuelling requirements with the race exhaust, then re-jetting (carburettor) or re-mapping (fuel injection) to suit.

If the machine is within its warranty period, note that should an engine-related problem occur after fitting an aftermarket exhaust system, the warranty may not apply. Check with your dealer if in doubt.

The materials used in the manufacture of exhaust systems are selected to give good durability, high temperature resistance and low weight. A light-weight system, whilst reducing the overall weight of the bike, will improve its braking and handling characteristics. Stainless steel is used for the header pipes where the exhaust temperature is at its hottest; a slight change in colour of the exhaust system is normal in this area.

Stainless steel is durable and resistant to corrosion. A stainless system will be lighter than a standard exhaust system.

Aluminium is used for header pipe flanges and various brackets. It is lightweight and easy to machine.

Carbon fibre has excellent temperature resistance, can be formed into heat shields and brackets, has good stiffness and is very light.

Titanium has high resistance to corrosion. It is much lighter than stainless steel but more expensive to produce.

Re-packing an exhaust can

Over a period of time the glassfibre wadding material will eventually start to burn away and the noise level will increase.

Materials can be purchased for re-packing exhaust cans. It is a relatively easy job to do, but does require the end cap to be detached; the end cap will be riveted, bolted or screwed into place and on some types of can you may need to remove both front and rear end caps.

Fitting a separate can

Carefully read the instructions and check you have all the parts and relevant tools. If the engine has been running allow time for it to cool down. The following procedure describes the fitting of a bolt-on can, with a slip-on fitment shown at the end of the sequence.

You are advised to keep the original exhaust and its mounting brackets, either for refitting when you sell the bike or if required to meet the requirements of the MOT test (i.e. if the aftermarket exhaust does not carry the 'BSAU' or 'E' mark and number). Note that some aftermarket cans (including road legal) may not pass the noise level check at a track day event.

1 Slacken the exhaust can upper mounting bolt.

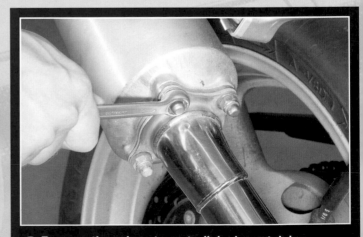

2 Remove the exhaust can-to-link pipe retaining nuts/bolts.

3 Remove the upper mounting bolt and withdraw the can from the bike.

6 Fit the exhaust can retaining nuts/bolts and finger-tighten them at this point.

4 Fit new gasket ring to the link pipe or exhaust can, depending on the type of fitment.

7 With the exhaust can in position, tighten all the mounting bolts securely.

5 Offer up the new exhaust can to the link pipe, align the mounting strap and secure with a bolt.

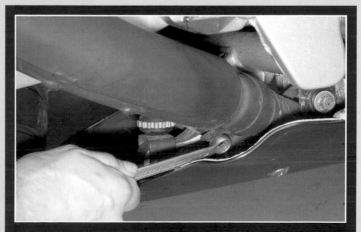

8 A slip-on can fitting has a clamp type attachment to the link pipe. Note that you may need to remove the lower fairing belly pan to gain access to the clamp bolt.

Fitting a high level can and link pipe

The fitting of an Arrow high-level exhaust can (road legal) is shown in the fitting procedure. The high level system requires the fitting of a new link pipe to enable the exhaust can to sit higher up on the machine. Note that such systems usually do away with the right-hand rear footpeg assembly, thus preventing the carrying of a pillion passenger.

On some machines with a variable valve in the exhaust system, the valve is incorporated in the link pipe rather than forward of the link pipe. In such cases, disconnect and remove the valve operating cables, but leave the servomotor operational.

Some later model bikes (e.g. R1, GSX-R1000, Fireblade etc.) have a valve in the exhaust system. When only changing the exhaust can and link pipe (not the complete exhaust system) the valve is not distrubed. When fitting a complete race system to a bike with an exhaust valve, leave the valve servo unit wired up and only remove the operating cables.

Carefully read the instructions and check you have all the parts and relevant tools. It is advisable to first assemble the new system off the bike so that you can identify which pieces go together.

Using a paddock stand lift the bike off the ground so that the exhaust system is accessible. If the engine has just been run, allow it to cool down before proceeding. Undo the retaining nuts/bolts and remove the standard exhaust can, then remove the rear footpegs from both sides of the bike. Remove the lower fairing panel, then undo their mounting bolts and withdraw the link pipe and end can from the bike.

NOTE

After fitting the exhaust system, check along the run of the system to make sure it is not touching the fairing panels or any other parts of the bike.

Run the engine and check that there are no exhaust gas leaks.

1 Fit the manifold to the exhaust valve housing, using a new gasket. Run the four bolts in finger-tight at first, making sure the two brackets are located correctly, then tighten all four bolts.

2 Smear some lubricating metal paste on the joints to help them slide together.

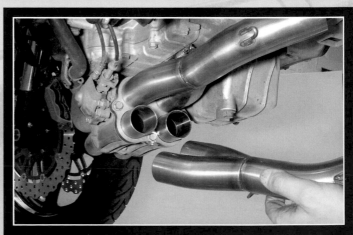

3 Offer up the two lower link pipes to the manifold, fit the upper section first and then the lower section.

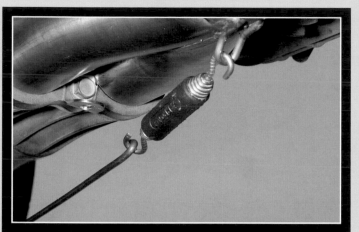

4 Secure the lower link pipes in place using a spring puller to hook the springs onto the brackets.

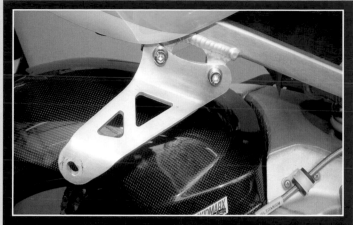

7 Fit the exhaust can mounting bracket, in place of the rear right-hand footpeg hanger.

5 Slide the middle section of pipe into place, making sure the mounting point lines up.

8 Slide the exhaust can onto the link pipe, align the mounting strap with the mounting bracket and secure with a bolt.

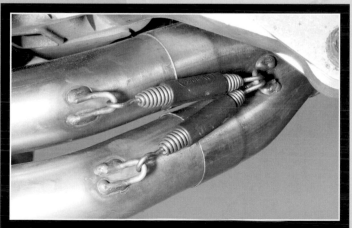

6 Secure the middle section to the lower link pipes using a spring puller to hook the springs into place.

9 Secure the exhaust can to the middle section link pipe using a spring puller to hook the spring into place.

Exhaust cleaning methods

Be careful what cleaning materials you use on the exhaust system. Avoid chemical cleaners or products which contain acidic additives.

On **stainless steel** components use a soft cloth sprayed with a contact cleaner to remove oil, grease and dirt, then wipe with a soft dry cloth (use polish to restore the original finish).

On **carbon fibre** components use a soft dry cloth to wipe off any dirt.

On **titanium** components use a soft cloth sprayed with a multi-purpose spray lubricant (WD-40 or equivalent).

Make sure the exhaust system has cooled down, before cleaning. Cleaning the exhaust system regularly cleaned will prevent spots from burning onto the surface. After cleaning the exhaust system, check that all bolts, clamps and springs are secure.

Removable baffle

Some exhaust cans have a removable baffle secured in the end of the exhaust can. The baffle may be held in place with a circlip, bolt or screw and also a spot weld. Note that the exhaust may be illegal if used with the baffle removed.

1 Use circlip pliers to remove the circlip . . .

2 . . . and allow the baffle to be withdrawn from the exhaust can.

Universal baffle kits (also known as Db killers) are available for most aftermarket exhaust cans. When inserted into the rear of the exhaust can, the noise reduction should satisfy noise regulation limits. A hole will need to be drilled in the end of the outlet pipe so that the baffle can be bolted in position.

Performance filters

Aftermarket performance air filters are designed to give excellent airflow, while maintaining high filtration levels to ensure long engine life. By replacing the standard air filter with a performance filter you can expect to increase the bike's power output.

The element of a performance filter is coated with oil to attract airborne dirt and dust particles. These particles are simply washed out during routine servicing and the element sprayed with the recommended filter oil for re-use. Performance filters may be more expensive than standard original equipment filters, but will prove more cost-effective in the long run.

Fitting

Performance filters are usually direct replacements for standard filters with no modifications required. The following procedure describes the fitting of a K&N performance filter to a Honda Fireblade.

Firstly, access the airbox, which on most superbikes will be under the fuel tank. Where possible, lift the fuel tank and support it using a metal stay. On some models you may need to disconnect the fuel lines and level sensor wires then remove the fuel tank completely; check your workshop manual for the correct procedure.

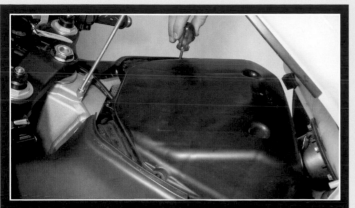

1 Work your way around the airbox cover and remove the retaining bolts. Some models may use spring clips.

4 Remove the new filter from its sealed plastic bag (the filter is supplied pre-oiled), then fit the filter into the airbox. Some filters will have specific fitting markings, such as UP or FRONT.

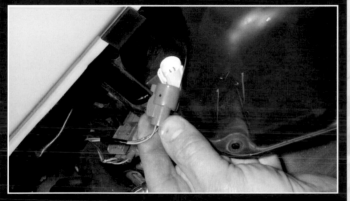

2 Disconnect any wiring connectors to the air temperature/pressure sensors located in the airbox cover.

5 With the filter located correctly, refit the cover and tighten the retaining screws evenly. On this filter cover there are also two screws located down the holes in its centre.

3 Lift the old air filter out of the airbox, then use a thin screwdriver to carefully prise out the filter's O-ring seal. Do NOT remove the O-ring which seals the upper and lower airbox sections.

6 Re-connect any sensor wiring connectors, then stick the performance filter sticker to the top of the airbox. This will ensure that when the bike next serviced, attention will be paid to the specific cleaning/re-oiling procedures. Refit the fuel tank and reconnect the fuel lines and wiring.

Fuel and ignition control

Any changes to the exhaust, air filter or other intake components will affect the engine's airflow. Unless this is compensated by adjusting the air:fuel ratio, the engine will not perform efficiently. On carburetted engines it may be necessary to "re-jet" the bike, and on fuel injected engines, re-mapping of the ECU may be required.

A slightly rich mixture is said to produce a smoother running engine, with less chance of engine damage. The theoretical ideal air/fuel ratio to ensure perfect combustion is 14.7:1, that is 14.7 parts of air to 1 part of fuel. However, in practice the ideal air/fuel mixture, for a normally aspirated engine, is around 13:1 air/fuel ratio. This will result in maximum power, optimum throttle response and good fuel economy.

If there is too much fuel (rich mixture), the ignition in the combustion chamber will be less efficient resulting in unburnt fuel being swept into the exhaust pipe and in extreme cases, leads to a risk of bore wash. If there is not enough fuel (lean mixture), the mixture will ignite early, risking detonation, causing reduced power and overheating

Dynojet kit

Fitting a Dynojet kit to a carburetted engine will increase power and smoothness throughout the entire rev range, whilst at the same time maintaining fuel consumption. Each kit includes full installation instructions, troubleshooting guide and all the necessary components, such as main jets and fuel needles. Various kits are available to suit the engine's state of tune:

Stage 1 jet kit – suitable for standard bikes fitted with standard or aftermarket exhaust and performance air filter utilizing the standard airbox (no other engine modifications). Improved running, better throttle response and a power increase of approximately 5% can be expected.

Stage 2 jet kit – suitable for standard to mildly-tuned engines using an aftermarket exhaust and a modified airbox. A power increase of up to 8% can be expected.

Stage 3 jet kit – suitable for standard bikes and tuned engines with a standard or performance exhaust and airbox replaced with individual filters. A power increase of 10% to 15% can be gained, although, the lower RPM is compromised slightly.

Stage 7 jet kit – designed for race applications and special applications only.

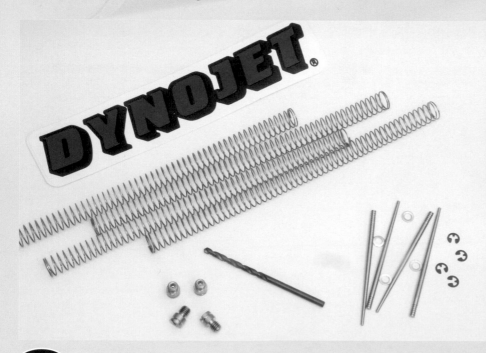

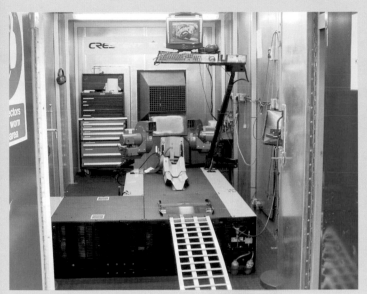

Typical dyno test station

The load control inertia dyno at work

Dynamometer

Dyno testing is utilized to examine how a bike is running by monitoring a range of data. If you intend fitting engine performance parts, a Dyno test performed before and after the modifications will show how they have influenced the power and torque curves as well as various other data channels. A dynamometer measures the engine output at the rear wheel, and charts power and torque curves in relation to engine speed. There are two types of dynamometers, inertia and "brake" dynos.

● An inertia dyno uses a heavy roller and corresponding system to measure various data channels. The Dyno calculates the engine's torque and power outputs by measuring the roller's acceleration. Most inertia dynos now incorporate load control to allow the user to place the bike under differing loads, and also allow the bike to be held at a set speed or rpm – this is a necessity for mapping fuel-injected machines.

● A "brake" dyno applies a brake load to the roller to hold the engine at a set rpm and measures a real-time torque; from this the bike's power can be calculated. This type of dyno is much less common.

You can prepare the bike for a dyno test by giving it a service; a new set of spark plugs, clean air filter and fresh oil – these measures can help achieve a true power and torque reading for the bike. The bike will be run at high speed throughout the rev range, so check that the tyres, chain and sprockets are

in good order. A chain which is badly adjusted or in need of lubrication could not only be dangerous, but will have a detrimental effect on the dyno reading.

Motorcycle dynamometers will be found at recognized test centres. One such scheme is the Dynojet Tuning centres – the accompanying photographs show the facility at Crescent Suzuki in Hampshire. The accompanying chart illustrates typical power and torque curves over the entire rev range. Maximum power and torque readings are stated, in this case 127.43 bhp and 66.74 ft-lbs. The Dyno also shows the air/fuel mixture over the rev range; in the read-out shown the engine is running slightly rich compared with the optimum setting.

DYNOJET Performance Evaluation Program

Dynojet WINPEP 7

DYNOJET RESEARCH — CF: DIN Smoothing: 5

RunFile_003.drf Max Power = 127.43 Max Torque = 66.74

Power (hp) vs *Engine Speed (RPM x1000)* / *Torque (ft-lbs)* / *Air/Fuel*

RunFile_003.drf - 22/04/2005 14:02:49 Run Type: RO Run Conditions: 80.50 °F, 29.99 inHg. Humidity: 17%, DIN 1.01
POWER RUN
Max Power = 127.43 Max Torque = 66.74
STD BIKE

Power Commander

The Power Commander is a "plug-in" device which fits "in-line" between the bike's ECU (electronic control unit) and the injectors. Therefore when the unit is removed the bike simply returns to standard. Whether the engine is in standard form or modified, once programmed, the unit is capable of setting the air/fuel mixture to ensure optimum performance and efficiency across the entire range.

The Power Commander stores a three-dimensional map of revs per minute (rpm) against throttle position and uses the programmed map settings to alter the injector pulse, in order to achieve the desired air/fuel ratio. These maps can be custom written, or for a bike with a simple configuration (e.g. a bolt-on exhaust with stock engine), the map can be downloaded from www.dynojet.co.uk or the CD-ROM provided with the Power Commander.

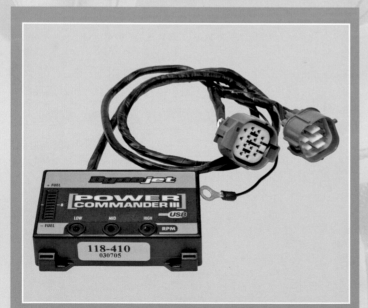

The Power Commander is a simple plug-in type of performance enhancement and as such can easily be disconnected and re-used on another bike. No permanent changes are made to the running of the bike – it will merely revert back to its standard settings.

The Power Commander has evolved through several different versions to the latest model, the Power Commander 3 USB. At the time of writing, there are only two models produced – the Power Commander 2 and the Power Commander 3 USB.

The Power Commander 2 fits before the bike's ECU and sends a modified signal from the bike's range of sensors, thus allowing the ECU to make the changes directly. The PC2 is now all but phased out with the exception of the Suzuki GSX-R750 2000-01 and the TL1000R models.

The Power Commander 3 USB has many more features. "Cylinder Trim" was utilised, allowing different amounts of fuel to be added to or removed from one or more cylinders, thus producing a smoother response especially on V-Twin engines. Its "Advanced Mapping" feature allows each cylinder to be mapped individually.

The development of the Power Commander 3 USB saw the map definition double, enabling fuelling to be controlled in 250 rpm increments as opposed to every 500 rpm. Its "Acceleration pump feature" can be enabled to allow a smoother transition between closed and open throttle. Another key advancement with the Power Commander 3 USB is the expansion port, which allows "add-ons", such as the Dynojet Quickshifter and ignition module.

Fitting

The Power Commander is supplied with all the components and information necessary to fit the unit as each one is tailored to fit a specific bike. The following procedure is provided as a guide and relates to the fitting of a PC3 (PCIII) USB to a Yamaha YZF-R1.

Begin by removing the seat units, then raise the fuel tank to access the injection system wiring harness; the fuel tank does not need to be completely removed. Temporarily locate the Power Commander inside the tail section and route the wiring towards the front of the bike.

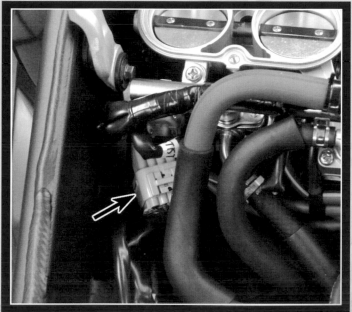

1 Locate the main wiring harness which runs to the injector rail and disconnect the wiring connector.

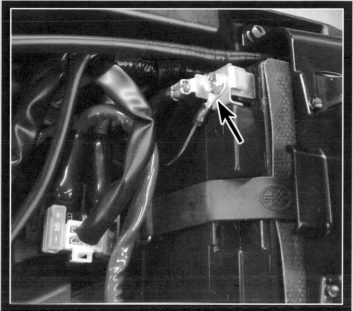

3 Connect the earth (ground) wire from the PCIII to the negative terminal of the battery.

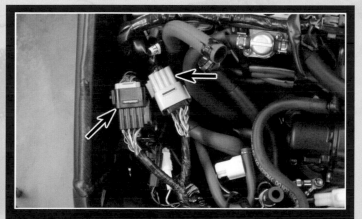

2 Plug the male connector from the PCIII into the female connector on the main harness and plug the female connector from the PCIII into the male connector from the stock injector harness. The injector harness connectors are grey and the power commander connectors are black.

Make sure the wiring from the PCIII under the tail section to the fuel rail harness is neatly routed and secured with cable ties.

4 The PCIII can now be secured to the inside of the tail unit using the Velcro pad supplied in the fitting kit. Refit the fuel tank and seat pads, taking care not to pinch any of the wires.

Suspension and Steering

When setting up suspension it is very important to understand how the adjusters affect the suspension action. If you are not sure what you are doing, leave adjustment to an expert; a few wrong adjustments could make the handling very dodgy with disastrous consequences.

On most superbikes the standard original equipment suspension units are of good quality and capable of dealing with normal road use. Aftermarket suspension units have a full range of adjustment features and although expensive, will improve the handling and give greater confidence for smoother riding.

Before making adjustment, check the bike over to ensure everything is in good working order. Check that the rear suspension linkage is operating smoothly and is not worn or in need of lubrication, that the front fork and rear shock oil seals are not leaking, and that the tyre pressures are correct. Always make a note of the current settings so

that you can revert to them if required. The manufacturer's base settings in the bike's owners manual will serve as a good starting point for setting up the suspension.

Remember that setting up the suspension for road use will most likely be a compromise between having a blast along open dry country roads and riding along a section of wet motorway with a pillion on board. Once you have found the ideal setting, stick to it, otherwise you could be altering it every weekend. Also don't assume that the suspension settings used by someone with the same model of bike will suit you and your bike – some riders are more experienced than others and have different riding styles.

Suspension adjustment

Pre-load

Spring pre-load adjustment involves setting up the suspension to suit the rider's weight. This will ensure that the suspension is in its optimum position (the middle third of its movement) when riding. The amount the suspension compresses from unladen (wheels off the ground) to laden (with the rider seated) is known as **sag**. Tightening the pre-load does not stiffen the spring, it alters the height of the bike to suit the weight of the rider, giving reduced spring travel.

It is important that the sag is measured, and altered if necessary by adjusting the pre-load, before any other suspension adjustments are made.

Static sag is the amount of movement from the suspension being fully extended (wheels off the ground) to the height at which the bike settles under its own weight.

Rider sag is the amount that the bike settles from being under its own weight to with the rider seated.

Spring sag is the distance the fork and shock compress from being fully extended (wheels off the ground) to with the rider seated.

Adjust front pre-load using the adjuster nut on top of the fork leg. Lines on the body of adjuster indicate pre-load position. Set each fork to the same position.

Adjust rear pre-load using the adjuster ring or collar on top of the spring. Use a round bar in the collar drillings to turn it. Other shocks have a slotted nut, often with a locknut, which can be turned with a C-spanner.

Measuring spring sag – stage 1

To be able to carry out these checks, you will need the help of a couple of friends to support the bike. The first reading taken will be with the weight off the suspension (unladen), so the wheels will need to be raised independently off the ground.

For the rear suspension check, if there are no specific markings on the tail unit as a reference point e.g. bolt, screw, transfer marking, use a piece of masking tape marked with a cross as shown.

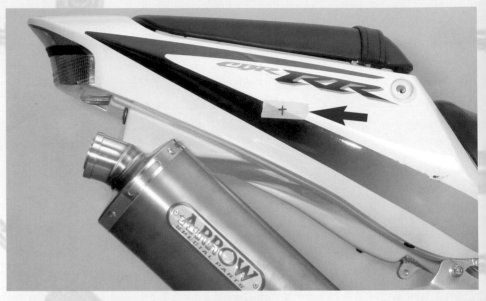

Pull the bike over on its sidestand to raise the front wheel off the ground. Measure the distance between the fork seal and the front wheel axle bolt on upside down (USD) forks. On conventional right-way-up (RWU) forks measure from the fork seal to the underside of the lower yoke. Record the measurement as 'A'.

Pull the bike over on the sidestand to raise the rear wheel off the ground. Measure the distance between the rear wheel axle bolt and a fixed point on the tail unit. Record the measurement as 'B'.

Measuring spring sag – stage 2

Repeat these measurements with the rider seated (wearing full bike gear) and both feet on the footpegs. The bike will need to be supported in the upright position with the help of an assistant. Allow the suspension to settle in its natural riding position with the rider's weight on it.

Measure the distance between the fork seal and the front wheel axle bolt on upside down (USD) forks. On conventional right-way-up (RWU) forks measure from the fork seal to the underside of the lower yoke. Record the measurement as 'C'

Measure the distance between the rear wheel axle bolt and a fixed point on the tail unit. Record the measurement as 'D'.

To calculate spring sag, subtract measurement 'C' from 'A' for the front sag reading, and 'D' from 'B' for the rear sag reading. Both readings should be approx. 30 to 35 mm. This figure is a good guide for road bikes. The sag should be a quarter to one third of the total suspension travel, so if the total travel is 120 mm the sag should ideally be 30 to 40 mm. For specific information on your model of bike consult the suspension manufacturer. On bikes used for racing the suspension will need to be stiffer, so the sag measurement will be around 20 to 25 mm. This again will vary depending on the circuit, riding style and bike model and will need to be determined by an expert.

NOTES ON SAG

- *When sitting on the bike to take the rider sag measurement it will be necessary to wear your full bike gear; the weight of full leathers, helmet, boots and gloves can make a significant difference.*
- *If you are not able to obtain the sag readings you require, the oil may require changing in the suspension units. Different springs with a harder or softer spring rate may also be required.*
- *Remember if most of your riding is with a pillion, the pre-load will need to be increased to stiffen the suspension.*
- *If the bike's suspension is too soft the pre-load needs to be increased. If it is too hard, decrease the pre-load.*
- *No matter how many times the sag is checked, each calculation will give a slight variation in reading. This is mainly due to the friction caused in the linkages and seals as the suspension is moved up and down. For a more precise reading, carry out these procedures twice, then take an average of the two figures.*

Compression damping

This controls the speed at which the spring can be compressed. When riding over uneven road surfaces, accelerating, braking or cornering, the spring rate needs to be controlled to keep the wheels in contact with the road.

Front forks

The front fork compression damping adjuster usually takes the form of a slotted-head screw at the bottom of the fork leg. The adjuster on each fork leg must be set to the same position.

Compression damping too soft – The bike will nose dive and bottom out, which could make the back wheel lose contact with the road and move out sideways. When braking into corners, the bike will nose dive and the bike will oversteer, making it turn in too quickly.

Compression damping too hard – The suspension will not compress quickly enough and the bike will skip along the road surface giving an uncomfortable ride and cause braking difficulties, especially in the wet. When braking into corners the suspension will be too stiff and the bike will understeer, drifting out wide on entry into the corner.

Compression damping too hard – The bike will skip along the road surface giving an uncomfortable ride and causing braking difficulties, especially in the wet. When accelerating, the rear suspension will not compress enough, causing the rear wheel to spin because of lack of traction. In extreme cases this could cause the wheel to kick out and throw you off the bike.

Rear shock

The rear shock compression damping adjuster is at the top of the shock and usually incorporated in the oil reservoir.

Compression damping too soft – When accelerating, the rear suspension will compress too much, causing the front end to lift. When accelerating out of a corner the front lifts and causes the bike to understeer and drift out wide on the exit.

Front suspension travel – quick check

This suspension travel check can be used as a guide to the correct compression damping setting for USD front forks.

Fix a cable tie around each fork leg slider (the shiny bit). Fasten them as near to the fork seal as possible, taking care not to scratch the slider's surface. Do not over-tighten the cable tie – it must be able to move on the slider as the suspension rises and falls.

Ride the bike and use braking, cornering and accelerating actions which typify your normal riding style.

With the bike at rest, check the distance between the cable tie and the fork outer tube casting. This distance represents the amount of front suspension travel. Ideally it should be no less than 15 mm, which will allow enough travel for any unsuspecting eventualities such as potholes, which could cause the suspension to 'bottom out'.

Note that this method can also be used to check the static sag and rider sag on USD front forks.

With the bike standing upright, under its own weight, fasten a cable-tie around the fork leg slider and move it up to the seal. Lift the front wheel so that the front suspension lifts to its full extent and measure from the cable-tie to the fork seal – this distance will be the **static sag**.

With the bike standing upright, under its own weight, fasten a cable-tie around the fork leg slider and move it up to the seal. Sit on the bike in full bike gear, then check how far the cable tie has moved down the fork leg sliders. Measure from the cable-tie to the fork seal – this distance will be the **rider sag**.

This indicates too much compression damping, causing the spring not to compress enough.

This is an ideal reading, allowing enough further movement for extreme conditions.

Not enough compression damping, causing the spring to compress too much and bottom out.

Rebound damping

Rebound damping is the opposite to compression damping; it controls the rate at which the spring returns to normal after it has been compressed.

Front forks

The front fork rebound damping adjuster screw is set in the centre of the pre-load adjuster at the top of the fork leg. Each fork must be set to the same damping position.

Rebound damping too soft – After the suspension has been compressed, it will come up too quickly causing the suspension to compress again giving a 'see saw' effect. If it rebounds too quickly when cornering it will cause the bike to understeer and drift out wide, resulting in a lack of traction.

Rebound damping too hard – The suspension will stay compressed for longer and will not react quickly enough to give the rider any feedback. When braking into corners, the bike will oversteer making it turn in too quickly.

Rear shock

The rear shock rebound damping adjuster ring is at the bottom of the shock (A). Note that this shock and many others incorporates a ride height adjuster nut and locknut (B).

Rebound damping too soft – After the suspension has been compressed, it will come up to quickly causing the suspension to compress again giving a 'see saw' effect. If it rebounds to quickly when cornering it will cause a 'wallowing' effect, resulting in a lack of traction at the rear wheel.

Rebound damping too hard – The suspension will stay compressed for longer and will not react quickly enough to give the rider any feedback. When accelerating out of a corner, as the front lifts, it will cause the bike to understeer and drift out wide on the exit, also resulting in a lack of traction at the rear wheel.

Rear shock upgrades

Aftermarket shocks can be very expensive, yet once set-up correctly can transform the handling of your bike.

The unit featured in the fitting procedure is a Nitron track shock which can also be used on the road. It is a light-weight unit consisting of titanium and anodised aluminium CNC (Computerised Numerical Control) machined components. When purchasing a new shock always read the instructions before fitting, paying particular attention to the maintenance and adjustment details. The shock will be pre-set with recommended settings; these are a guideline only and may need to be altered to suit the rider. For example, if you are 16 stone it may be set too soft, if you are 10 stone then it may be too hard.

Fitting

You may need to remove the rear wheel, exhaust, seat unit and/or battery tray to access the shock mountings. A paddock stand which fits under the swingarm will not be suitable for this job as the swingarm needs to be free to move freely; the bike will need to be supported using a frame mounted stand which allows the rear wheel to be lifted off the ground.

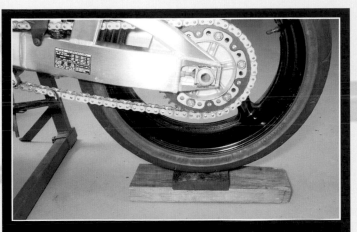

1 Use blocks of wood under the rear wheel to raise it to the correct height for removing the suspension mounting bolts.

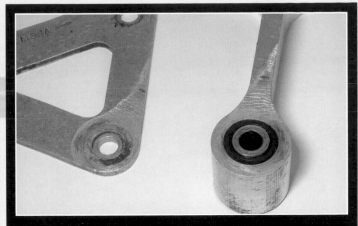

4 With the suspension linkage off the bike, check for wear in the components. Note the scuffing on this link arm and plate.

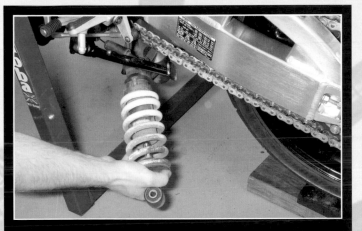

2 Follow the procedure in the workshop manual to remove the old shock from the bike.

5 Check and lubricate the suspension linkage bearings. Renew any worn bearings and always fit new seals.

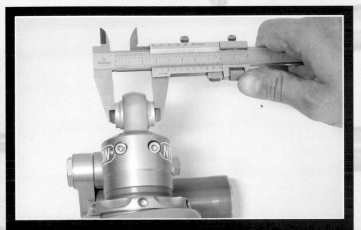

3 Compare the mounting point dimensions of the new and old shocks.

6 Follow the workshop manual fitting procedure, tightening the mounting bolts to their specified torque settings. Also note any specific installation instructions provided with the new shock.

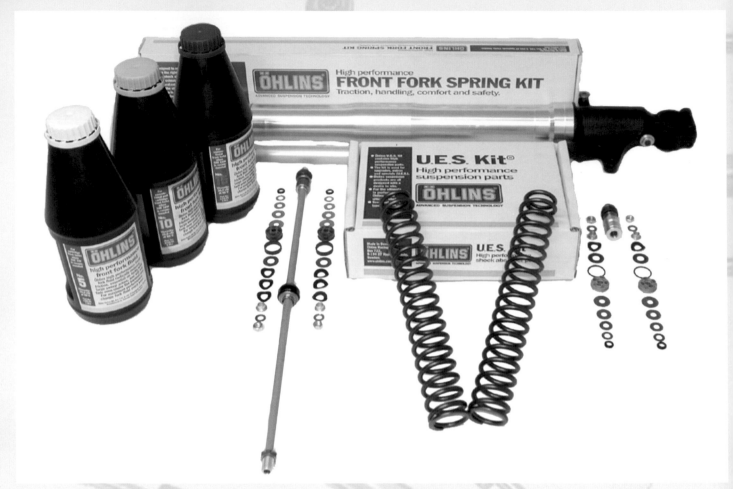

Front fork upgrades

Fork springs

There are different types of springs available for front fork legs. Most superbikes have either dual-rate springs or progressive springs fitted as standard. Spring rate is measured as the resistance a spring gives to being compressed. This rate is measured by how much force it takes to compress the spring by 1 inch. If the pitch (gap) between the coils is constant (single rate spring) then so is the rate. The tighter wound coils of a dual-rate or progressive spring will compress with less force than the wider spaced coils.

Single-rate springs (linear) have the same pitch (gap) between each coil over its full length. These are commonly used by performance tuning experts because the coils compress at a more predictable fixed rate.

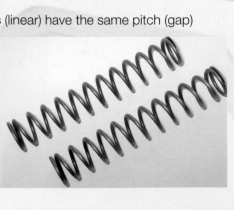

Dual-rate springs have tighter wound coils at one end of the spring. As the spring is compressed the coils which are wound tighter together close up first as they have a lower rate.

Progressive springs have the coils at different pitches (gaps) all along the length of the spring. As the suspension is compressed, this gives a smooth increase in spring rate.

Aftermarket springs are usually about 10% to 15% stiffer than original springs. Replacing fork springs is a relatively easy job and can be carried out with the aid of a workshop manual. Depending on the type of fork fitted, you may need special tools – always check beforehand.

When the springs are renewed always renew the fork oil and top-up to the correct level. The oil is an important part of the front suspension so make sure the correct viscosity and quantity of oil is used.

Re-valving

If a change of fork oil and new springs fails to improve the fork action, you could consider having the fork damper units re-valved. This will cost much less than buying a new set of Öhlins or WP forks and enable the front suspension to be set-up to suit your riding style, weight and type of use (racing, touring, fast road, track days etc.). This job is best left to an expert as it requires special equipment and techniques that can only be performed by a suspension specialist. This type of work can also be carried out on the rear shock.

Swingarms

A braced or single-sided swingarm will make your bike stand out from the rest. Aftermarket braced swingarms are bigger, stronger and lighter than original equipment fitments, and available in upper braced, lower braced or upper and lower braced forms. Specialist companies will make up swingarms to your requirements, such as required for drag racing where you need those extra few inches.

Check when buying if pivot shaft bushes and bearings and the wheel axle are included with the swingarm.

Chain adjusters come in different forms but are usually either slotted adjusters or eccentric adjusters. This aftermarket chain adjustment set-up is manufactured by Harris and used in Superbike racing.

If you are on good terms with the bank manager, then why not go for a mirror polished single-sided swingarm. Metmachex offer the complete package which includes Dymag rear wheel, carbon fibre hugger, Brembo caliper and bracket, brake hose, sprocket and carrier, axle and single nut wheel fixing including safety clips.

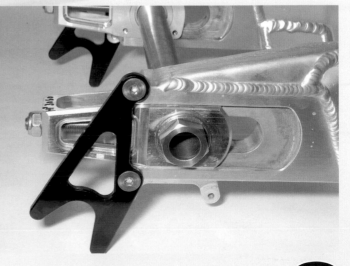

Steering dampers

If you have ever had the misfortune of experiencing a "tankslapper", you will appreciate the need for a steering damper.

With the performance of modern superbikes, it is inevitable that when accelerating hard the front wheel is going to lift. As the wheel touches back down on the tarmac and is out of alignment with the rear, there will be some tyre deflection causing it to bounce to one side and here begins the "tankslapper". Even if the front wheel does come down in the straight-ahead position (in line with the back wheel), if the road surface is uneven the result will be the same. Without a steering damper, the tyre deflection can cause the handlebars to flap from left to right with great force, taking them out of your hands with disastrous consequences. A steering damper will dampen out the deflections as the tyre bounces from side to side and help keep the front wheel in a straight line. Because of the steering geometry used on most modern superbikes a steering damper is often fitted as standard, but these units are not usually adjustable.

Aftermarket steering dampers can have up to 28 position settings which provide a progressive range of damping force. Most are light-weight, completely re-buildable and fully adjustable.

Steering dampers are available in different lengths and a variety of colours to suit your bike. Not only do these look

trick, but they are an essential item for stability and handling.

Most dampers require a fitting kit to suit the exact model of bike. Some aftermarket steering dampers replace the standard steering damper so will not require a fitting kit.

A side-mounted steering damper is illustrated here, although there are other mounting variations such as the 916 style/across, behind headlight, under bottom yoke and original mount; check which is suitable for your bike.

OHLINS STEERING DAMPER KIT

A steering damper is not fitted as standard to all bikes. In such cases the steering geometry is designed to give quick handling without compromising the stability needed to dampen out any oscillations. On some bikes, the steering geometry can be altered so as not to require a steering damper, although such adjustments should only be made by a suspension expert.

Fitting

The fitting of a 28-position Gubellini steering damper is illustrated in the following procedure. Whichever damper is being fitted, always read the fitting instructions thoroughly and check that all the components are supplied before proceeding. Position the bike on a level hard standing, preferably held upright on a paddock stand.

3 Slacken and remove the steering stem nut.

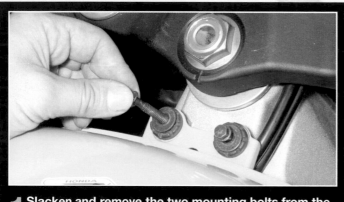

1 Slacken and remove the two mounting bolts from the front edge of the fuel tank.

4 Locate the upper yoke bracket over the steering stem, making sure the lugs on the underside of the bracket are positioned at the back of the yoke. Fit the new retaining nut and tighten it to the correct torque setting.

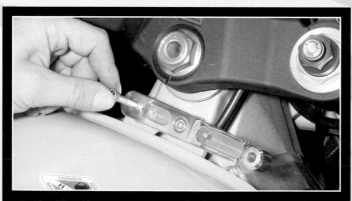

2 Position the bracket from the fitting kit across the front of the fuel tank mounting point and tighten the mounting bolts. Use thread-locking compound on the bolt threads.

5 Fit the steering damper clamp to the upper yoke bracket, using the bolt provided in the fitting kit along with the spacer and O-ring. Take care not to damage the O-ring as the bolt is tightened. Use thread-locking compound on the threads of the bolt.

6 Slacken the two clamp bolts and slide the steering damper through the clamp from the left-hand side.

9 Slide the damper into position and tighten the clamp bolts (torque setting supplied with instructions).

7 Bolt the damper rod end to the mounting bracket using the retaining bolt and spacer from the fitting kit. Note any position markings described in the fitting instructions.

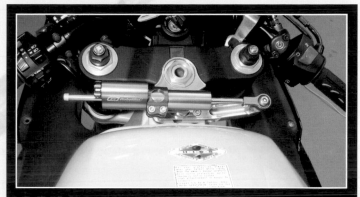

10 Position the steering in the straight-ahead position and check that a similar amount of damper rod is showing at each side. Turn the steering from lock to lock and check the damper does not go to its full travel on either lock. If the damper travel exceeds its range the steering damper and fitting kit could be damaged.

8 Use thread-locking compound on the threads of the bolt and tighten it securely.

CAUTION

● Check that the steering damper does not foul on anything, e.g. screen brace, top yoke, fork legs, pre-load adjusters (see photo), handlebars, brackets, etc. On side-mounted dampers, always check the clearance from your knee to the damper as the steering is turned.

● Always ride with care when taking the bike out for its first test ride after fitting the damper. We advise the damper be on a low setting initially, then gradually increased to the desired damping setting when you have become used to its action.

Brakes

The most powerful part of your bike is the brakes, or it should be. The engine puts out a lot of power, accelerating the bike from 0 mph to 100 mph very quickly, but the brakes should take you from 100 mph to 0 mph quicker. A recent test report gave these findings:

	0 to 100 mph	100 to 0 mph
Yamaha R1	6.8 sec	5.3 sec
Suzuki GSX-R750	6.4 sec	5.3 sec
Kawasaki ZX-10R	5.8 sec	4.5 sec

Much effort is put into increasing engine power, yet little consideration is given to upgrading the braking system. When increasing the power of the engine, you need to increase the stopping power of the brakes.

There is plenty of choice when it comes to brake components and not only do these parts improve braking power but they also look trick. Wavy discs, also called contour discs or petal design, braided hoses and a radial front master cylinder are desirable items to fit.

Pads

When fitting new pads to aftermarket discs, determine which pad compound will be the most suitable; if necessary refer to the disc manufacturer for advice.

Note that it is usual practice to use standard organic pads for the rear brake and sintered-metal pads for the front brake. This is because the rear brake is not used as much as the front and does not therefore require that extra bite afforded by sintered pads; it could get you into serious trouble by locking up the rear wheel!

There are four main types of brake pads for road use:

Organic pads use materials like Kevlar and fibreglass (asbestos is no longer used). They work well at low temperatures, have a good braking effect with little lever effort and are quiet when applied. Under constant heavy braking, however, they can overheat causing rapid pad wear, brake fade and oxidization. Suitable for both cast iron and stainless steel brake discs.

Semi-metallic pads contain elements of sintered brass, iron or bronze. They are a high performance brake pad with a very long pad life. Suitable for stainless steel brake discs only.

Full-metallic pads are made from sintered brass, bronze, copper or a mix of metals with very little binder. They have good stopping power and work to a high temperature, but usually require more lever effort. Suitable for stainless steel brake discs only.

Carbon pads for road use are semi-metallic pads that have powdered carbon added to them to improve the varied temperature properties. The disadvantages are that they are expensive and leave a residue of black, sticky, brake dust around the wheels and calipers. Suitable for both cast iron and stainless steel brake discs.

PAD FACTS

- *Hard compound pads can increase disc wear rate, especially when used on standard (original equipment) discs.*
- *Always replace the pads in both front calipers at the same time, never just one side.*
- *Full braking power will not be available until the pads have been run in. Treat the brakes gently for the first 100 miles.*
- *When fitting new brake discs, always fit new brake pads.*

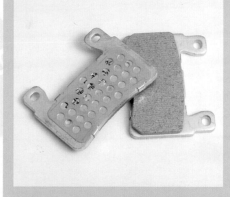

- *The grill on the rear of this pad is a stainless steel radiator plate which reduces the heat transfer into the brake's hydraulic system.*
- *When fitting brake pads a copper-based grease or similar should be applied to the backs and sides of the brake pad metal backing.*

Brake fluid

Regular brake fluid changes are often overlooked and only considered when renewing the hoses or working on the calipers or master cylinder.

Brake fluid should be changed at least once every 12 months to keep it up to spec. If the bike is not used over the winter period, and is left in a cold damp environment, then the fluid should ideally be changed before the bike goes back on the road. Glycol-based brake fluids are hygroscopic, which means they absorb water from the air, lowering the boiling point quite considerably.

Glycol-based fluids are rated as DOT 3, DOT 4 and DOT 5.1 and are all compatible with each other. The DOT 5 rating is a silicone-based fluid and MUST NOT be mixed with any glycol-based fluids. Check which rating is suitable for your bike before use – it is usually printed on the reservoir cap.

The typical "dry" boiling points for the glycol-based fluids are:

DOT 3	220°C
DOT 4	260°C
DOT 5.1	275°C

DOT 5 silicone fluid is used as standard in very few motorcycles. It is coloured purple to distinguish it from the glycol fluids. It has the advantage of a longer life span and if spilt will not damage paintwork. The disadvantage is that silicone does not absorb water, so any water which gets into the system sinks to the bottom which means it ends up in the calipers; this is not good for the boiling point or corrosion resistance. DOT 5 silicone fluid requires different composition seals than used in a glycol fluid system, so apart from not mixing the fluid types, do not use DOT 5 in a system designed for use with glycol-based fluid.

CAUTION

- *Always use clean fresh brake fluid when renewing or topping up the brake fluid. Do not shake the bottle before use as this will cause the fluid to get air bubbles.*
- *Always take care when using glycol-based brake fluids (DOT 3, DOT 4 and DOT 5.1) because any spillage will damage paintwork and plastics. Flush the area immediately with plenty of water if spillage occurs.*

Discs

The following procedure illustrates the fitting of EBC floating contour discs to the front and a solid contour disc to the rear. The front discs have a lightweight gold-coloured forged alloy centre hub. The periphery of the discs is of a profiled contour "wavy" design to reduce weight and improve the braking effect. As the disc rotates, the wave design helps it cool down quicker and also has a self-cleaning effect.

Fitting a rear disc

Slacken the rear wheel axle retaining nut with the wheel resting on the ground. Now use a paddock stand to lift the rear wheel off the ground so that the wheel can spin freely. Remove and refit the rear wheel using the correct method, referring to a workshop manual.

CAUTION

Always make sure the wheel is fitted correctly; refer to the workshop manual for details. Note that new pads must be fitted with new discs.

1 Slacken and remove the disc retaining bolts, then remove the old disc from the wheel.

3 Note any markings on the face of the disc. This arrow indicates the direction of rotation.

2 Clean around the seating area. If this is not free from dirt the disc will not sit squarely on the wheel.

4 Fit the new disc to the wheel. Apply thread locking compound to the retaining bolts, then tighten them evenly and in a diagonal sequence to the correct torque setting.

Fitting front discs

Slacken the front wheel axle retaining nut/bolt whilst the wheel is resting on the ground. Now, using a front paddock stand, lift the front wheel off the ground so that the wheel can spin freely. Remove the front wheel using the correct method, referring to a workshop manual; note that in most cases you'll need to detach the calipers first.

Coloured fasteners can further improve the look of new discs – titanium spec is advised. Here gold-coloured disc bolts and axle bolt replace the standard items.

1 Slacken and remove the disc retaining bolts, then remove the old disc from each side of the wheel.

2 Clean around the seating area. If this is not free from dirt the disc will not sit squarely on the wheel.

3 Fit the new disc, making sure that any markings on the face are facing the correct way. Some discs are handed (only fit on the left or the right side), check for markings or a directional arrow.

4 Apply a non-permanent thread locking compound to the disc retaining bolts.

5 Tighten the bolts evenly and in a diagonal sequence to the correct torque setting.

6 Turn the wheel over and repeat the procedure for the disc on the other side of the wheel. Use blocks of wood to support the wheel so that the disc on the opposite side of the wheel will not be damaged.

Braided hoses

Braided hoses consist of a stainless steel braiding over a PTFE/Teflon hose. Their main advantage is in improved braking feel and control, but they also look better than the standard fitment brake hoses too. The HEL hoses shown in the fitting procedure have titanium fittings, banjo unions and bolts. Titanium is lighter than steel and also has excellent corrosion and water resistance.

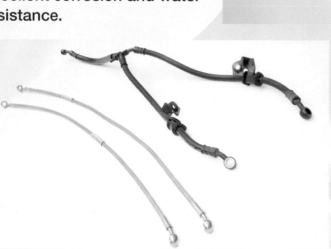

When purchasing replacement brake hoses, most people opt for a two line set-up to replace the three line original. This eliminates the T-connector under the lower yoke, reduces weight and provides a more even braking. A double banjo bolt will be required to connect the two hoses to the master cylinder.

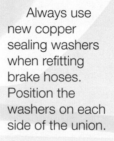

Always use new copper sealing washers when refitting brake hoses. Position the washers on each side of the union.

When removing the original brake hoses, note their routing for refitting. Also check the length of the new brake hose in comparison with the old one.

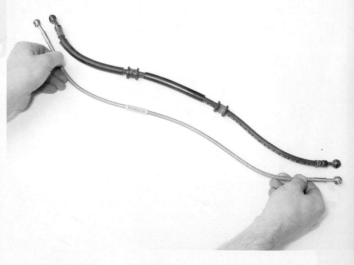

The banjo unions on the end of the brake hoses are available at different angles; check they match those of the original hose.

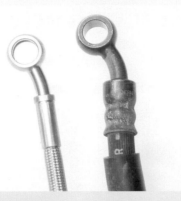

Fit separators along the length of the brake hoses to prevent them rubbing against bodywork, fork legs and the bottom yoke.

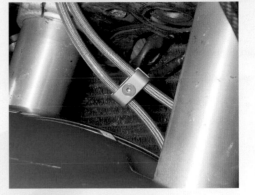

Make sure the brake hose is positioned at the correct angle. Abutments (lugs) on the caliper and master cylinder are usually provided to locate the neck of the banjo union correctly.

Braided hoses have a clear heat shrink plastic coating to provide weather protection and to prevent damage to plastic body panels. Braided hoses with coloured PVC protective covers are available to complement your bike's paintwork.

New bushes will be required to support the new brake hoses in their mounting brackets. If necessary, remove those from the original rubber hose and use them to secure the new hose.

Fit new P-clips to secure the front brake hoses to the mudguard. You'll need to form the P-clip into the correct shape. Ensure the rubber strips seat correctly to prevent chafing.

Most manufacturers also offer a range of stainless steel fittings in various colours.

WARNING

DO NOT use aluminium fittings (anodised or plain) for road use, these are for competition use only and are not road legal. When two metals (in this case stainless steel and aluminium) with different galvanic potential are placed together corrosion can take place. This could lead to brake failure with disastrous consequences.

Radial front brake master cylinder

The radial master cylinder is used in every level of motorcycle racing throughout the world because it allows the rider to use less energy at the brake lever, which enables more sensitive braking.

On a standard master cylinder the piston is parallel to the brake lever, whereas on a radial master cylinder the piston is perpendicular to the brake lever; this improves the feel of the brake and gives excellent stopping power.

A Brembo 19 x 20 radial master cylinder is illustrated in the fitting procedure. Its size specification means that it has a 19mm bore and is 20mm from the fulcrum and point of support to the piston rod. There are various sizes available, but the most common are the 19 x 20 for twin front disc brakes and the 16 x 18 for a single front disc brake. The span of the lever is also adjustable to suit the rider's needs.

Fitting

Drain the old brake fluid from the front brake system.

1 Place cloth under the banjo bolt union at the master cylinder to stop any fluid dripping onto paintwork, then slacken and remove the banjo bolt.

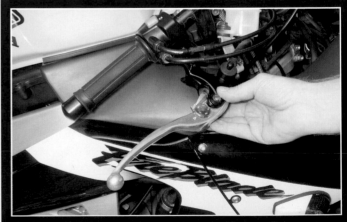

2 Undo the two mounting bolts and withdraw the master cylinder complete with reservoir from the handlebar. Disconnect the wiring connectors from the brake light switch as it is removed.

3 Fit the radial master cylinder to the handlebar and tighten the two mounting bolts. Note the arrow pointing upwards.

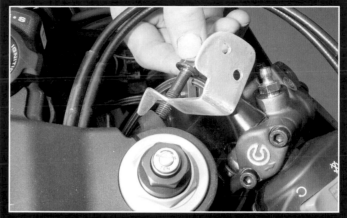

6 In this case the reservoir mounting bracket was attached to the top yoke fork clamp bolt. Check steering movement to ensure that the reservoir doesn't foul any components.

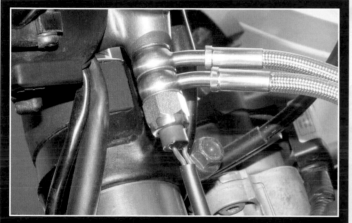

4 Fit the new banjo bolt/brake light switch, using new sealing washers on the brake hose connections. Re-connect the wiring for the brake light.

7 Mount the reservoir to the bracket and connect the hose to the master cylinder. Fill the system with fresh brake fluid and bleed the system of air.

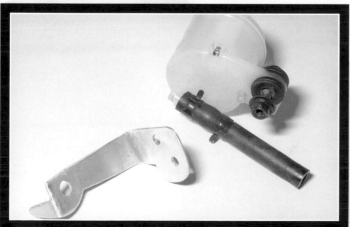

5 The reservoir does not mount directly to the master cylinder like the standard one – a mounting bracket will have to be made to mount the reservoir.

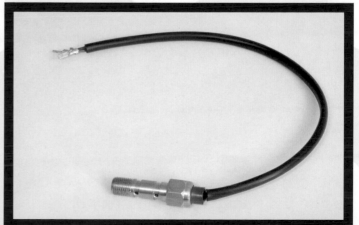

8 The radial brake master cylinder does not have provision for a conventional brake light switch. You will need to obtain a pressure activated switch set into the head of the hose banjo bolt.

Bars and Controls

Ever bought the bike of your dreams only to find the riding position does not suit your height and riding style? Aftermarket clip-ons and rear sets are the answer and most types provide a range of adjustment.

Some clip-ons and rear sets have very little, or no adjustment, and you'll need to check their distances and angles beforehand to ensure they will be suitable. Fully adjustable clip-ons and rear sets, although more expensive, will enable you to achieve the most comfortable riding position; they will also give you the option of alternative positions, say for track day use where additional ground clearance is required.

Clip-ons

What are clip-ons and why use them?

Clip-ons are special handlebars which clamp around the fork legs to provide a lower and generally more forward riding position than offered by the original bars. They are ideal for track day use because they enable a more crouched riding position and handling is improved due the rider's weight being further forward.

Hinged or two-piece clip-ons are recommended where the clip-ons fit beneath the top yoke. This will prevent having to remove the top yoke or drop the fork legs if you need to remove them in the future. It is important that the diameter of the handlebar tube on the clip-ons is the same diameter as the original handlebar in order to accommodate the switches, throttle tube and other controls.

Check the angle of the bars in relation to the clamp – clip-ons are available at different angles to suit your requirements. Race style clip-ons are usually adjustable and once fitted to the bike can be positioned to suit your riding style.

Race clip-ons do not have provision for the handlebar switch locating peg. Having determined the correct angle and location for the switch, mark the position of the locating peg and drill the bar to accommodate the peg.

Certain models have a threaded hole in the original handlebar to mount the brake/clutch fluid reservoir bracket. When fitting race clip-ons you will need to make up a new bracket or modify the original bracket to mount the reservoir. See the Brake chapter for further information on moving the brake fluid reservoir.

To remove the original handlebars you will need to remove the top yoke or drop the fork legs – refer to the workshop manual for further information. After fitting clip-ons, make sure the steering can be turned from side to side without the handlebars fouling other components or contacting the fuel tank when the steering is on full lock. Check that all wiring, cables and hydraulic lines to the controls are correctly routed and not strained at any point.

Bar grips

Replacement bar grips are available in many different materials and colours, some with heater elements. Most are suitable for bikes with 22mm (7/8 inch) diameter bars. Those shown in the fitting procedure are made from a soft density rubber with a choice of different coloured inner sleeves.

3 Clean the handlebar to make sure it is free from dirt, then lubricate it with a smear of washing-up liquid. This will help the new grip slide on and stay in place once fitted. If the grip is not secure glue may be needed.

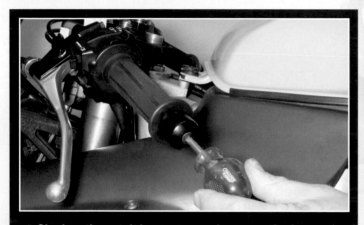

1 Slacken the retaining screw and remove the bar end weights.

4 Slide the grip onto the bar. Where the grips have a moulded name or inscription, take care to position this so that it reads correctly (not upside down) and that both sides align with the throttle grip at rest.

2 Work a screwdriver between the bar and grip, then spray penetrating oil inside to aid removal of the old grip. Be careful not to damage the plastic throttle tube when removing the throttle grip. If the grip is stuck fast, cut it with a knife and peel it off the bar.

5 Refit the bar end weight and tighten it securely. Note the fitting of crash protector end weights to this bike. On the throttle grip side, check that the end weight doesn't restrict throttle rotation – the throttle grip must snap closed when released.

Rear sets

What are rear sets and why change them?

Rear sets are complete rider footpeg and rear brake/gearchange lever assemblies which are mounted further back and higher than original units. They will give a more comfortable riding position with increased ground clearance. Most rear sets have a range of adjustment.

Always read the fitting instructions thoroughly and check that all the components are supplied before proceeding. Note that heel guards are not always included in the kit – check with the supplier and if necessary purchase these separately or re-use the original ones.

Make sure the bike is on a level hard standing before any work is carried out. Ideally position the bike upright on a rear paddock stand to allow full access to each side and the rear wheel to be rotated for checking gear selection and rear brake operation.

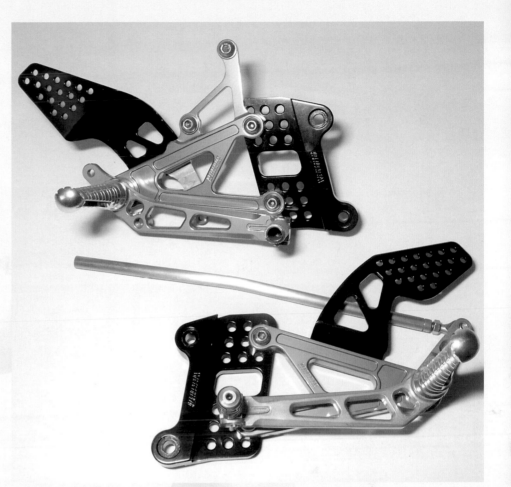

It is advisable to first assemble the rear sets on the bench and familiarise yourself with how they fit together. Do not use any thread lock at this stage.

During assembly use copper grease on the footpeg shaft at the point where it passes through the gear lever and brake pedal pivots.

Fitting the right-hand rear set (brake pedal side)

Once the rear set assembly has been fitted, check the position of the brake pedal and brake master cylinder linkage. Make sure they do not contact the frame, fairing, swingarm or any other component during operation. A small amount of brake pedal height adjustment is possible via the locknut and adjuster nut on the master cylinder pushrod.

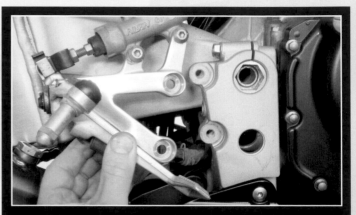

3 Withdraw the footpeg hanger from the bike.

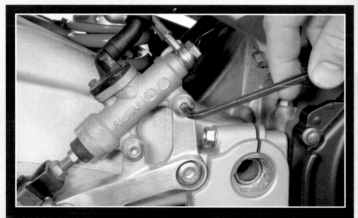

1 Slacken the master cylinder mounting bolts – these also secure the heel guards on most models.

4 Remove the split-pin and clevis pin from the brake master cylinder linkage.

2 Slacken and remove the footpeg hanger mounting bolts.

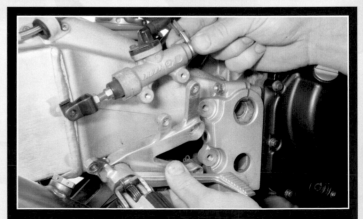

5 Remove the mounting bolts and secure the brake master cylinder safely to prevent straining the brake lines.

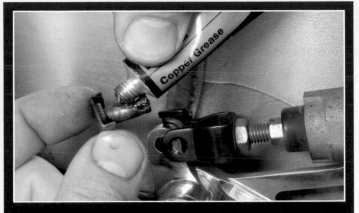

6 Withdraw the footpeg assembly and disconnect the brake light switch from the bracket.

9 Using copper grease on the clevis pin, reconnect the brake master cylinder linkage to the brake pedal. Use a new split-pin to secure the clevis pin.

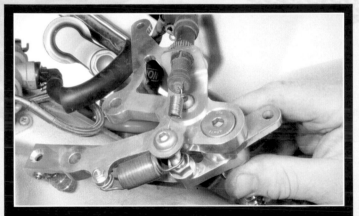

7 Offer up the rear set assembly and re-connect the brake light switch. Leave adjustment of the switch until all components are in place.

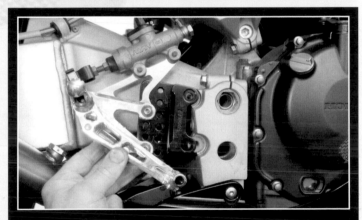

10 Install the rear set assembly and fit the mounting bolts finger-tight as this stage. Press the brake pedal a couple of times to check the brake operation.

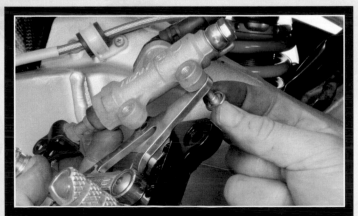

8 Align the brake master cylinder and refit the mounting bolts.

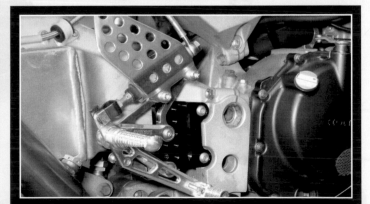

11 Once the position of the rear set has been established, remove the mounting bolts one at a time, apply a few drops of non-permanent thread lock to their threads, then tighten them securely. Adjust the brake light switch setting.

Fitting the left-hand rear set (gear linkage side)

Once the rear set assembly has been fitted, check the position of the gear lever and linkage rod. Make sure they do not come into contact with the frame, fairing, sidestand or any other component while being operated through the gears. Note that fine adjustment of the gear lever height can be made via the linkage rod – tighten the rod locknuts afterwards.

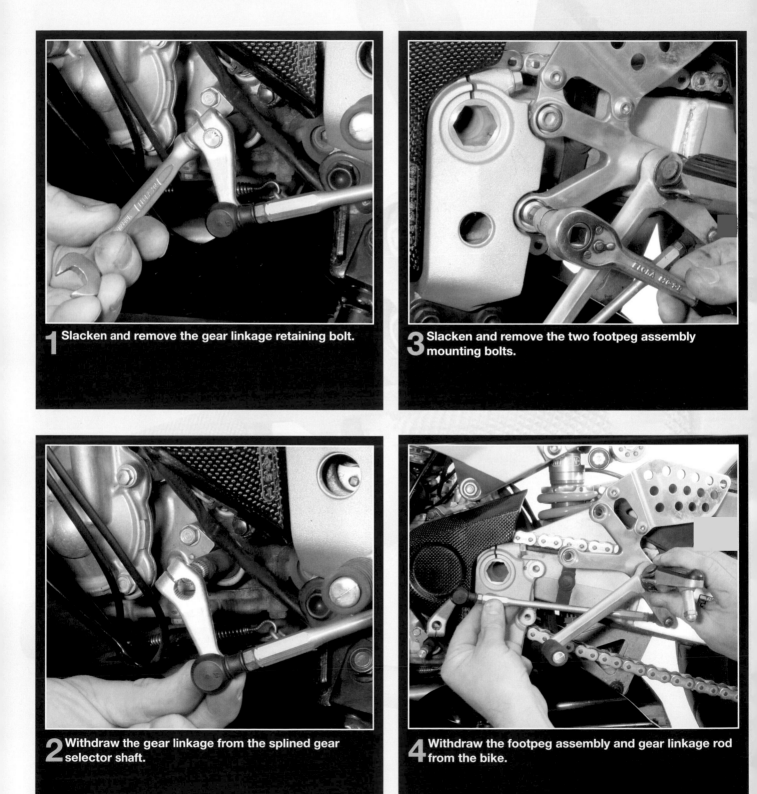

1 Slacken and remove the gear linkage retaining bolt.

3 Slacken and remove the two footpeg assembly mounting bolts.

2 Withdraw the gear linkage from the splined gear selector shaft.

4 Withdraw the footpeg assembly and gear linkage rod from the bike.

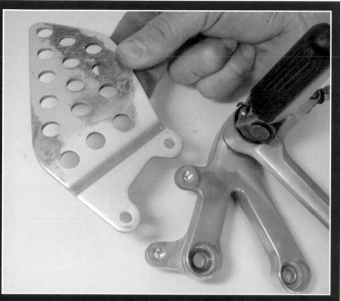

5 Unbolt the heel guard from the footpeg mounting bracket if you are going to re-use them.

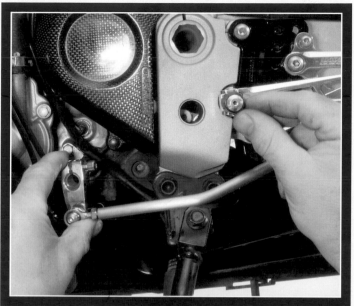

7 Align the gear lever in the position you require, then slide the gear linkage bracket onto the splined gear selector shaft.

6 Offer up the new rear set assembly up to the bike and fit the mounting bolts finger-tight at this stage.

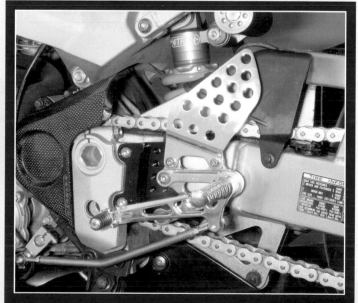

8 Once the position of the rear set has been established, remove the mounting bolts one at a time, apply a few drops of non-permanent thread lock to their threads, then tighten them securely.

Hydraulic brake light switch

If it proves difficult to fit the original brake light switch, spring and mounting bracket to the new rearset assembly, perhaps due to there not being a suitable position to mount the switch, you could consider an hydraulic switch.

The hydraulic brake light switch will eliminate the original switch, spring and brackets and simply replaces the existing banjo bolt in the master cylinder.

After fitting the switch, bleed the rear brake circuit of any air and top up the fluid reservoir if necessary. If any brake fluid was spilt during this procedure, use plenty of water to wash it off.

1 Slacken and remove the banjo bolt from the master cylinder. Be prepared for brake fluid loss - place a cloth under the banjo bolt to catch fluid spills.

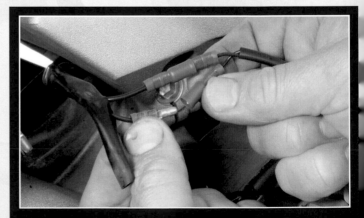

3 Either disconnect or cut the wiring to the original brake light switch.

2 Thread the hydraulic brake light switch into the master cylinder in place of the banjo bolt, using new copper washers on each side of the banjo union.

4 Fit new wire terminals and connect the wiring to the hydraulic brake light switch.

Jack-up plates

If rear sets are out of your price range consider fitting jack-up plates. They comprise two mounting plates which are pre-drilled with a number of holes to re-mount the standard footpeg hangers. Note that when moving the standard footpeg hangers further back adjustment of the gear linkage rod length will be required – check that a linkage extension is supplied.

When fitting the jack-up plates ensure that the brake pedal and gear lever do not foul on other components.

The term 'jack-up plates' also refers to alternative suspension linkage plates used to change the ride height of the bike – make sure you state exactly what is required when ordering!

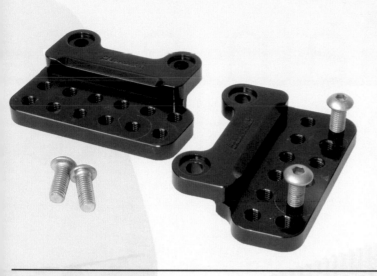

Heel guards

Heel guards are fitted to prevent the rider's foot contacting moving parts, such as the chain, rear wheel etc. They are however, in a fairly exposed position and will become scuffed over a period of time. Complement rear sets with a new set of heel plates; they are produced in many different designs and materials, colour-anodised or with laser-cut inscriptions.

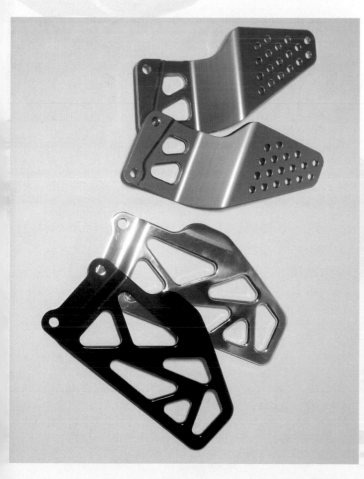

Original equipment aluminium heel plates can be given a new lease of life by having them polished.

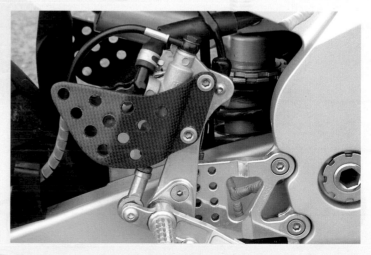

Carbon fibre heel guards are lightweight, strong and look trick.

Chain and Sprockets

One of the most important parts on your bike is the chain and sprockets. There's no point having masses of torque at the transmission output shaft yet expect worn sprockets and a badly adjusted chain to transmit this efficiently to the rear wheel.

Whether you use your bike for commuting, track days, attending bike shows and rallies or just for those Sunday ride-outs with your mates, always check out the best set-up for you. Look in any catalogue or bike magazine and you'll see that there are many chain and sprockets options to suit your bike. Decide what it is you want. Is it looks, altered gear ratio for performance, long life span, or maybe all of these? Always aim to buy the best quality products you can afford.

On the bike shown, we are fitting a steel Renthal front sprocket (one tooth down from standard), a Supersprox "Stealth" rear sprocket and an Afam gold link "X"- ring chain. Check with your supplier and find out what is suitable for your bike. Depending on your requirements, they may even be able to suggest the best chain and sprocket set-up.

Front Sprocket

The precision CNC (computer numerical control) manufactured sprocket shown is made from Nickel Chrome Molybdenum steel; it's case-hardened to give strength and hardness, and thus plenty of mileage. There is also an option for lightened sprockets which have been drilled.

The original 16-tooth sprocket is being replaced by a 15 tooth sprocket. This will give better acceleration, but on the down side will lose a bit of top speed. For a bike with a top speed of about 165 mph this will mean losing about 10 mph; I can't see that being a problem, can you!

You can get the same effect by fitting a larger rear sprocket; for every one tooth down on the front sprocket, the nearest equivalent would be to increase the rear sprocket by three teeth (see *Gear Ratio*).

If the speedo is driven by the transmission, then altering the gearing will give you a false reading at the speedo. For example, by reducing the front sprocket from 16 to 15 teeth, an indicated speed of 100 mph on the speedo, in truth would be about 94 mph ($15 \div 16 \times 100 = 93.75$).

"Out of sight, out of mind"

Most front sprockets have covers fitted, so cannot be seen. Remove the front cover to check the condition of the front sprocket as this is usually the one that gets neglected. While the cover is off, this is a good time to clean out the grease and dirt that has built up around the casing.

Rear Sprocket

The Stealth Supersprox rear sprocket shown, is said to last twice as long as quality steel sprockets and three times longer than aluminium sprockets. It also has the added bonus of looking trick, with the coloured alloy inner section.

So why is it called STEALTH ?

STE = Steel (outer teeth section)

AL = Aluminium (inner section)

T = Teeth (New tooth design)

H = High performance

Lightness is achieved by making the inner section of aerospace aluminium which is CNC machined. The steel outer toothed section has a new tooth design, with grooves between the teeth to allow dirt to escape; this prevents damage to the chain and sprocket, so making them last longer.

If it's looks you are after, then there are many companies making anodised alloy sprockets in various colours.

Chain

There are many different makes and types of chain available. Unless you are using your bike for racing or regular track days, the common sizes for sports bikes are 530 or 525 chain. An Afam super heavy duty "X" ring 530 chain with gold links is shown in the accompanying photo sequence. Remember that if you are fitting a different front or rear sprocket (less teeth or more teeth) then you may need a different length chain to that specified for the original fitment.

If you are using your bike for racing or track days, then the 520 chain and sprocket set up is desirable. It is used in racing because it is lighter but more importantly that there are more sizes of sprocket available for this size of chain, which will give you the gearing you require depending on the race circuit. The 520 chain is a narrower gauge than the 525 and 530, which means it is lighter.

Fitting

While the bike is still on the ground, slacken the rear wheel axle retaining nut, then remove the front sprocket cover and slacken the front sprocket retaining bolt/nut. Using a paddock stand lift the rear wheel off the ground so that the wheel can spin freely.

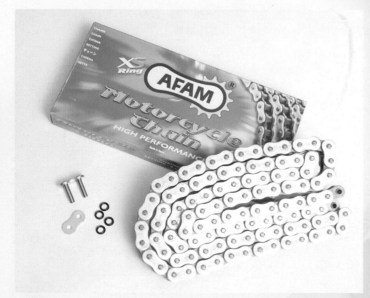

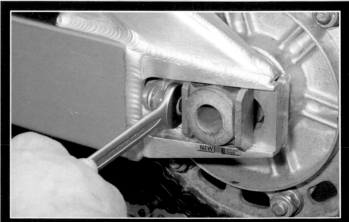

1 Slacken the chain adjusters on both sides of the swingarm and slide the wheel forward; this will create slack in the chain

2 Lift the chain off the rear sprocket, withdraw the wheel axle and remove the rear wheel. You will need to support the rear brake caliper and its bracket as the wheel is removed.

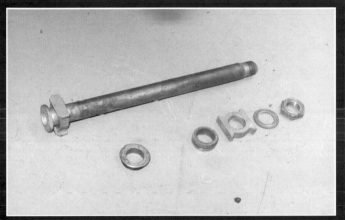

3 Make sure the axle and spacers from each side of the wheel are kept safe and in the correct order for refitting.

4 Slacken and remove the rear sprocket retaining nuts and washers, then remove the rear sprocket from the wheel.

5 Clean around the seating area. If this is not free from dirt then the sprocket will not sit squarely on the wheel.

6 Fit the new rear sprocket making sure that any markings on the face of the sprocket are facing outwards.

7 Tighten the retaining nuts to the correct torque setting.

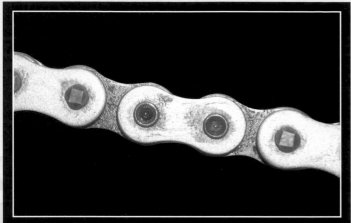

8 The soft link can be identified by finding the two pins that are different from the others; these are normally a different colour and look as if they have been centre-punched.

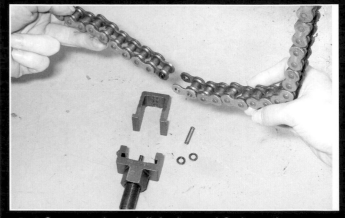

11 Separate the soft link pins and O-rings, then remove the chain from the bike.

9 Remove the old chain, you will need a chain splitter to press out the pins of the soft link - do not use any other tool.

12 Remove the front sprocket bolt or nut.

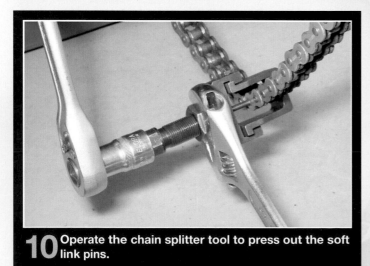

10 Operate the chain splitter tool to press out the soft link pins.

13 Withdraw the sprocket from the transmission shaft. Note that some bikes have a lock washer.

14 Refit the new front sprocket with its markings facing outwards. Tighten its retaining bolt/nut to the correct torque setting. Intall the rear wheel.

17 Fit the O-rings to the soft link pins. Use the chain tool to press the side plate into position, then to rivet the pin ends.

15 Fit the new chain around both sprockets so that its ends are in the middle of the bottom run.

18 Ensure the soft link pins are riveted securely.

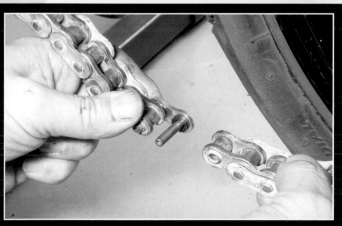

16 Fit the new soft link, with its O-ring seals, through the chain ends.

19 Lube and adjust the new chain. Check that wheel alignment is correct.

	FRONT SPROCKET					
	13	**14**	**15**	**16**	**17**	**18**
48	3.69	3.43	3.20	3.00	2.82	2.67
47	3.63	3.36	3.13	2.94	2.76	2.61
46	3.54	3.29	3.07	2.88	2.71	2.56
45	3.46	3.21	3.00	2.81	2.65	2.50
44	3.38	3.14	2.93	2.75	2.59	2.44
43	3.31	3.07	2.87	2.69	2.53	2.39
42	3.23	3.00	2.80	**2.63**	2.47	2.33
41	3.15	2.92	2.73	2.56	2.41	2.27
40	3.08	2.86	2.67	2.50	2.35	2.22
39	3.00	2.79	2.60	2.44	2.29	2.17
38	3.92	2.71	2.53	2.38	2.24	2.11

(REAR SPROCKET — left axis label)

Sprocket markings :
TG442 - Part number
17T – Number of teeth
(525) – Specification

Gear Ratio

This is probably the cheapest and easiest way to alter the bike's power delivery to suit your riding. Changing the ratio between the front and rear sprockets can have a significant effect on performance.

The normal ratio with standard sprockets (e.g. 16 / 42) is 2.63. This means that the front sprocket has to turn 2.63 times to one complete turn of the rear sprocket. The table shows that going down one tooth to 15 on the front sprocket gives a 2.80 ratio with the standard 42 tooth rear sprocket. To achieve an equivalent ratio by changing the rear sprocket, it would be necessary to go up three teeth to a 45 tooth rear sprocket whilst retaining the standard 16 tooth front sprocket, thus giving a gear ratio of 2.81.

Chain care

Adjustment
Running an overtight chain is far worse than it being a bit loose. An overtight chain will increase the running temperature which in time will stretch the chain and wear the sprockets. In extreme cases the chain could snap and cause extensive damage to the underside of the bike and to the engine lower cases! With the rider's weight on the bike the suspension movement increases and the chain tightens. So a fairly tight chain adjustment when the bike is on its stand with no rider seated, becomes effectively tighter when in use.

Conversely a loose chain will cause the chain to "ride up" into the weaker upper part of the sprocket teeth and curl the ends of the teeth. It will eventually slip around the sprocket taking the top of the sprocket teeth off. It will also wear away anything in its path as it is flapping around, such as the swingarm, frame or casings.

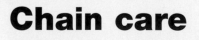

Lubrication

Lack of lubrication is a common cause of chain and sprocket wear. The chain must be lubed at regular intervals. If the chain is dirty, then before lubricating, clean it using a suitable degreaser and soft brush, when the chain has dried it can then be lubricated.

Wheel alignment

When adjusting the chain always make sure the tensioners on each side of the swingarm are adjusted equally. With the bike on the stand, look down the run of the chain and spin the wheel. The chain should run in a straight line and not snake from side to side. Poor alignment will wear the sprockets and affect the handling.

CAUTION

It is not advisable to fit a new chain if the existing sprockets are worn or to renew the sprockets if the chain is worn out – the new component will wear at a greater rate than if the chain and both sprockets were renewed as a set.

Chainguards

Black plastic chainguards usually fitted as standard original equipment can be replaced with aftermarket items made from aluminium, stainless steel, carbon fibre or fibreglass. There are many anodised colours available including polished or chromed finishes and some designs also incorporate laser-cut inscriptions.

Certain designs of rear hugger incorporate a chainguard and obviate the need for a separate component. See the Bodywork chapter for details.

For a bike to be road legal it must have a form of chainguard fitted. Apart from catching any chain lube flung off the top run of the chain, its fitting is important for two safety reasons.

● If the chain breaks or a sprocket fails, the chainguard will take the initial impact minimising any injury to the rider or passenger.

● In the case of an accident the chainguard will help prevent the rider's or passenger's legs coming into contact with the chain and sprocket.

Aftermarket chainguards are a direct replacement for the standard item and will simply attach to the existing mounting points.

Tyres and Wheels

Tyres

Motorcycle tyres have a relatively small footprint area (contact with the road surface) compared with other vehicles and as such their correct selection is essential to ensure good traction and handling. Sports tyres will give good grip and reasonable mileage for road use, whereas the more 'sticky' performance sports tyres provide maximum grip albeit at a higher wear rate.

Spend time making the tyre choice. As well as the bike manufacturer's tyre recommendations, seek advice from motorcycle tyre fitting specialists, refer to tyre manufacturer's catalogues, and read the many tyre tests conducted by the motorcycling press. Ensure that the tyres you select are suitable for your bike – certain tyres, although of the correct size, will have specific uses such as those designed for heavy-weight touring bikes. Bear in mind that tyre manufacturers develop their tyres to work as a matched pair, front and rear.

Tyre sidewall markings

The tyre sidewall contains information relating to tyre construction, dimensions and intended application.

The essential piece of information is the size marking. Two typical size markings are shown. The tyre section width is measured at its widest point and expressed in millimetres. This is followed by the aspect ratio, which is the height of the tyre expressed as a percentage of the section width.

120/70ZR17 m/c (58W)

120	Section width (mm)
70	Aspect ratio
Z	Speed symbol or rating
R	Radial construction
17	Rim diameter (inch)
M/C	Motorcycle use
58	Load index
W	Speed index

190/50ZR17 m/c (73W)

190	Section width (mm)
50	Aspect ratio
Z	Speed symbol or rating
R	Radial construction
17	Rim diameter (inch)
M/C	Motorcycle use
73	Load index
W	Speed index

The arrow on the tyre sidewall should follow the direction of normal wheel rotation. This is because the tread pattern is designed to work in one direction only. Ensure the arrow is pointing in the correct direction when the wheel is fitted to the bike.

Some front wheels have a directional arrow, which must also follow the direction of normal wheel rotation.

Tyre speed symbol (rating)

The speed symbol letter indicates the maximum sustained speed possible. This assumes that the tyre is fitted to the bike and rim design for which it was intended, is inflated to the correct pressure and operating within its load index rating. Note that a reduced load index usually applies if a tyre is used at very high speed.

	Max. mph	Max. kph
V	149	240
(V)	over 149	over 240
W	168	270
(W)	over 168	over 270
Z	over 149	over 240
Y	186	300

Tyre load index rating

The load index relates to the maximum axle load that the tyre can carry. In the examples shown overleaf, a load index of 58 equates to an axle load of 236 kg and the 73 load index equates to a 365 kg axle load. A full load index table will be found in tyre manufacturers' literature, whereas those relevant to superbikes are included here.

LI	Kg	LI	Kg	LI	Kg	LI	Kg
40	140	66	300	53	206	79	437
41	145	67	307	54	212	80	450
42	150	68	315	55	218	81	462
43	155	69	325	56	224	82	475
44	160	70	335	57	230	83	487
45	165	71	345	58	236	84	500
46	170	72	355	59	243	85	515
47	175	73	365	60	250	86	530
48	180	74	375	61	257	87	545
49	185	75	387	62	265	88	560
50	190	76	400	63	272	89	580
51	195	77	412	64	280	90	600
52	200	78	425	65	290	91	615

Tyre maintenance

Check the tyre pressures weekly and always when the tyres are **cold**. Incorrect tyre pressures will result in poor handling, irregular tyre wear and can also lead to tyre damage. Refer to the owners manual or the tyre label on the swingarm or chainguard for recommended pressures. Pressures will be given in psi or Bar – see the converter chart.

Make sure there is no chain grease or oil on the rear tyre.

Check for bulges and lumps from internal damage to the tyres.

Remove any stones that may be stuck in the tyre treads.

Keep an eye on the tread depths.

Pressure converter chart

Bar	psi	Bar	psi	Bar	psi
1.2	17	1.9	28	2.6	38
1.3	19	2.0	29	2.7	39
1.4	20	2.1	31	2.8	40
1.5	22	2.2	32	2.9	42
1.6	23	2.3	34	3.0	44
1.7	25	2.4	35	3.1	45
1.8	26	2.5	36	3.2	46

Tyre and Rim fitments

e.g. J17XMT6.00

J17   Wheel diameter in inches

MT   5° taper on the bead seat

6.00   Rim width in inches

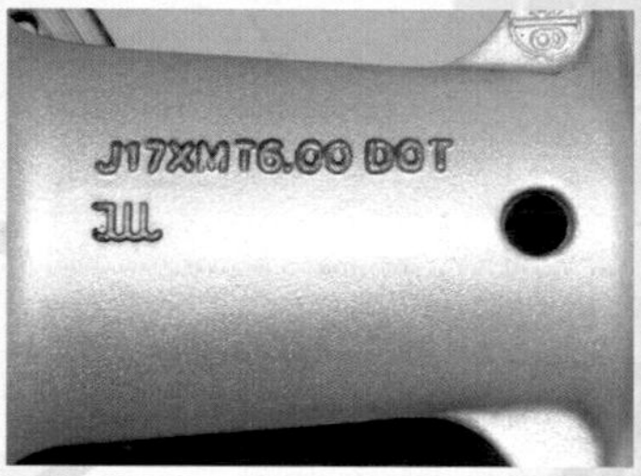

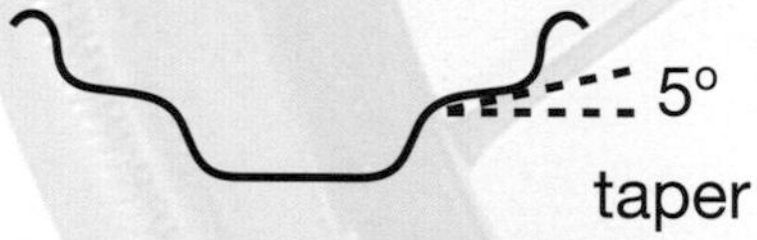

5° taper

Most bikes use an MT contour rim, which has a 5° taper on the bead seat. The accompanying charts are a guide to the radial tyre size fitment options for MT rims. Note that the recommended fitments are in bold.

60, 65 and 70 aspect ratio tyres

Rim width (inch)	Tyre width (millimetres)			
6.50	230			
6.25	200	**230**		
6.00	200	230		
5.50	170	180		**200**
5.00	160	170	**180**	
4.50	140	150	**160**	170
4.25	140	**150**	160	170
4.00	130	140	150	
3.75	120	130	**140**	
3.50	**120**	**130**		
3.00	**110**			

80 and 90 aspect ratio tyres

Rim width (inch)	Tyre width (millimetres)		
4.50	160	170	
4.25	160	170	
4.00	150	160	**170**
3.75	140	150	**160**
3.50	130	**140**	150
3.00	110	120	
2.75	100	110	**120**
2.50	90	**100**	110

50 and 55 aspect ratio tyres

Rim width (inch)	Tyre width (millimetres)		
6.50	200		
6.25	**200**		
6.00	180	**190**	200
5.50	**180**	190	

Running-in new tyres

Exercise extreme caution for the first 100 miles on new tyres. This will allow sufficient time for the components of the tyre (carcass, belts, tread strip, rubber mix etc.) to bed-in and the tyre to seat fully on the wheel. The surface of new tyres is very smooth and will need to be scrubbed-in. During this 'scrubbing-in' period vary the angle of lean so that the tyre will scrub-in evenly and avoid hard braking and rapid acceleration. If you are doing this during the winter season you may need to allow at least 200 miles to run the tyres in.

After the running-in period check the tyre seating and pressures, then gradually increase the acceleration and braking forces.

CAUTION

Remember that tyres need to reach operating temperature before they work to their best efficiency and give maximum grip.

Wheels

The materials commonly used in the manufacture of wheels are aluminium, magnesium and carbon fibre. All these materials are light-weight, strong, rigid and have a good resistance to oxidisation. Fitting lighter wheels will reduce the gyroscopic effect, which will improve the handling, making turning into corners easier. Also lighter wheels will accelerate faster and stop quicker as there is less mass to rotate.

Compared with standard original equipment wheels, the weight saving of fitting aftermarket wheels is likely to be up to 25% for aluminium wheels, up to 45% for magnesium wheels, and up to 65% for carbon fibre wheels. Refer to wheel manufacturers' catalogues for precise details of the wheel saving per model. For example, one wheel producer has indicated the following weight reduction between aftermarket and original equipment alloy wheels:

	OE wheel weight	Aftermarket wheel weight	Weight saved	Percentage
Honda CBR900RR	9300	7600	1700	18.2%
Kawasaki ZX-9R	10,400	7800	2600	25.0%
Yamaha YZF-R1	9700	8100	1600	16.5%
Suzuki TL1000R	9800	8100	1700	17.3%

Wheel types

There are many designs and colours available, depending on the style you are looking for, ranging from 3 spoke to 10 spoke. Composite wheels are available, such as those with an alloy rim and magnesium spokes and hub, and those with a carbon fibre rim and magnesium spokes and hub. Some wheels are supplied with bearings, seals, spacers, rear sprocket, disc bolts and tyre pressure valve - check when purchasing.

A cheaper alternative to new wheels is to have the standard wheels re-finished. There are many options available, from painted, powder coated, polished, anodised and chromed.

The wheels can be further enhanced with rim transfers, either around the periphery of the rim or at the spoke roots – see overleaf.

Wheel rim transfers

Add finishing touches to the wheels with rim transfers. These are available as a stripe designed to run around the rim periphery or decals to apply at equidistant points around the rim or at the spoke roots. Many rim transfer colours and designs are available.

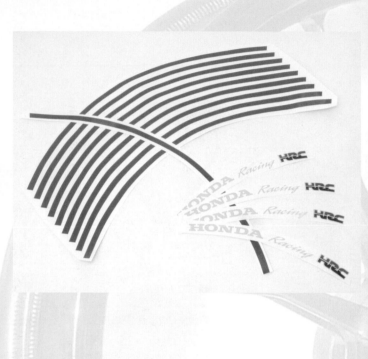

2 Peel the backing paper off part of the stripe and carefully place the stripe in the desired position on the wheel rim.

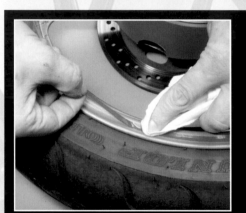

3 Working your way along the stripe remove the rest of the backing tape and smooth it down into position.

Rim stripe fitting

Remove the wheel from the bike for ease of working and clean the rim area thoroughly.

The stripe is fitted in four sections to make up the full circle. The sections are designed to overlap by a few millimetres to ensure that the join doesn't show and the kit will usually come with a couple of spare sections to allow for any fitting errors.

4 When starting the next stripe, overlap the first piece by about 2mm.

1 Use a dry cloth to clean all dirt from the wheel rim. Tar spots and chain lube can be removed with a dedicated wheel cleaner.

5 With all four pieces fitted, carry out the same procedure on the other side of the wheel.

3 Working your way along the decal smooth it down, making sure no air has been trapped.

Rim decal fitting

It's not essential to remove the wheel from the bike to fit decals, although you may find it easier to clean the rim thoroughly and space out the decals evenly with the wheel on the bench.

   Clean the rim area and dry it with a soft cloth. Remove any tar spots and chain grease with a dedicated wheel cleaner.

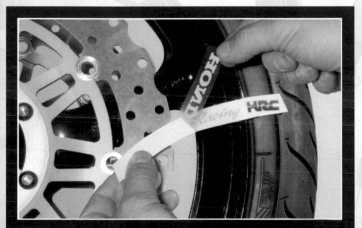

1 Peel the backing paper off the decal, making sure all the decal stays on the application tape.

4 Remove the application tape by peeling it back on itself, keeping it close to the rim.

2 Carefully place the tape in the desired position on the wheel rim.

5 Follow the same procedure to fit a decal to the other side of the wheel.

Bodywork

Screens

The most popular aftermarket screen for superbikes is the double bubble (airflow) type. It is used in racing because it greatly improves airflow over the rider. It also enables a better view of the instruments due to it being higher than the standard screen.

All aftermarket screens, where applicable, are pre-drilled and can simply be fixed to the original screen mountings. Road and race screens differ in thickness - approximate material thicknesses are 3mm for road screens and 1.5mm for race screens.

Screens are available in a wide range of colours, including iridium, smoked, silver and stealth finishes. Note that a clear screen is advised for racing because it enables clear vision when the rider is tucked down over the tank.

Standard factory-fitted screen.

"Flip up" screen as used for sports tourers.

"Double bubble" screen. Otherwise known as an airflow screen.

Screen fixings

Screen fixing kits are available in a wide range of colour anodised or titanium fasteners. If a new fixing kit is not available the wellnuts will

need to be removed from the old screen and re-used. Wellnuts made from a soft rubber are easily removed, whereas those made from a harder material require a different technique:

Soft rubber wellnuts

1 With the retaining screw removed, the outer part of the soft rubber wellnut is on the outside of the fairing panel. These are normally the factory-fitted original type.

2 The wellnuts will remain inside the mounting holes in the screen; they can easily be pushed out.

3 Thread the retaining screw into the nut by a couple of turns. Push the screw and wellnut into place. A smear of lubricant will aid installation of the wellnut.

4 Tighten the retaining screw and check that the wellnut has spread on the inside of the fairing to hold the screen securely.

Hard rubber wellnuts

1 Run the screws back into the wellnuts by a couple of threads while they are still in the screen.

2 Press down on the head of the screw until the threaded nut part of the wellnut is pushed back down to the bottom of the rubber sleeve.

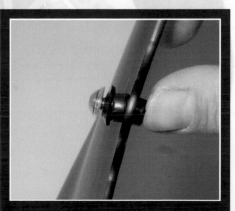

3 With the screw still in the wellnut, press against the bottom of the rubber sleeve and push it out from the screen.

Screen fitting

Note that on certain models it will be necessary to remove trim panels from around the instruments and fairing and to remove the mirrors in order to access the screen fixings.

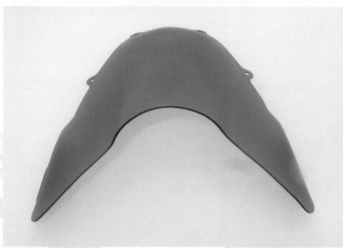

Screen trim is available in a number of colours to suit your bike.

1 Press the wellnuts into the mounting holes in the new screen.

4 Tighten the screws at the front lower part of the screen first, then work back along the screen tightening the other screws. Take care not to over-tighten them.

2 Clean around the fairing, then slide the new screen into place, taking care not to scratch its surface.

3 Align the wellnuts with the holes in the fairing and fit the screws with the washers supplied in the fixing kit. Run all the screws in by hand first to make sure they locate correctly.

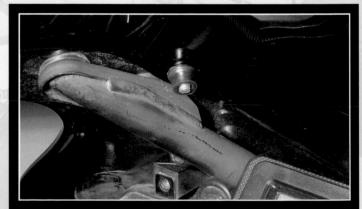

5 Check the inside of the screen to ensure the wellnuts have spread out to hold the screen securely.

Tank pads

A tank pad will protect the tank from scratches caused by the zips and buckles of your jacket. Tank pads are available in many different styles, colours and materials to suit your bike; some companies will create personalised tank pads bearing your own design. Most types have an adhesive backing and are easy to fit.

Heat can be used to remove an existing tank pad of the plastic type. Carefully heat the tank pad using a hot air gun and peel it from the tank. Be very careful not to hold the hot air gun too close to the tank – gentle heating is all that is required to soften the adhesive. Do NOT use a hot air gun on a plastic fuel tank.

Fitting a carbon fibre tank pad

2 Use the cleaning wipe in the fixing kit to remove any dirt and grease from the tank surface.

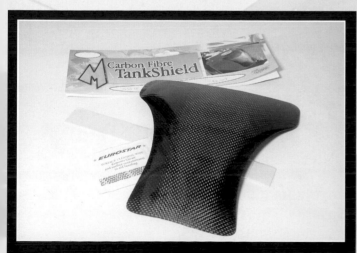

1 The fitting kit contains a number of adhesive pads to attach the pad to the fuel tank. The tank pad is pre-formed into the shape of the tank and each type is thus model-specific. In addition to the carbon fibre pad shown, other materials used are Kevlar, aluminium and titanium.

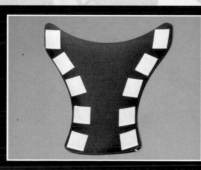

3 Remove the backing tape from the adhesive pads and stick them to the rear of the tank pad. Make sure they are spaced out equally on the outer edges.

4 Peel the facing from the other side of the adhesive pads, then align the tank pad in the centre of the tank and press it firmly into place.

Fitting a gel-filled tank pad

The Motografix tank pad shown is a 3D gel-filled pad which is resistant to fading.

3 Peel back the backing sheet from the bottom of the tank pad and centralise it at the base of the tank.

1 Clean the tank surface to remove all traces of dirt and grease.

4 Peel off the rest of the backing sheet, then align the tank pad in the centre of the tank.

2 Using a piece of string as a guide, mark a line down the centre of the fuel tank with a non-permanent felt pen.

5 Use a clean cloth to smooth out the tank pad and press it firmly into place.

Fuel caps

A flush-fitting race-style fuel filler cap will add the finishing touch to your modified bike. Most caps are made from a lightweight high quality aluminium, although titanium caps are also available. There is usually a choice of colours, including natural alloy and polished finishes.

Aftermarket fuel caps are a direct replacement for the standard cap, although being a race type product they have a quick release operation and are non-lockable.

Fitting a race style cap

1 Using an Allen key, remove the standard fuel filler cap retaining bolts.

2 Insert the key into the fuel lock cap and lift the assembly out of the fuel tank. Note on some models there may be a vent pipe connected to the base of the assembly.

3 Clean inside the aperture before fitting the new race fuel filler cap.

Fitting replacement cap bolts

Merely replacing the bolts of the existing filler cap can add a splash of colour to the bike. Most aftermarket bolt suppliers produce packs of bolts for this purpose.

1 Using an Allen key, remove the fuel filler cap retaining bolts.

4 The filler cap will only fit in one position; align the mounting holes as you seat the cap in place.

2 Working your way around the fuel filler cap, replace the old bolts with the new anodised retaining bolts. Compare the length of the new bolts to the ones you remove, before fitting.

5 With the new filler cap in place, tighten the retaining bolts securely.

3 With all the bolts in place carefully tighten them down. The bolts are aluminium so do not over-tighten them.

Undertrays

An undertray will create a more streamlined look to the back end and dispense with the fairly ugly standard rear mudguard extension. Undertrays are also known as tail guards or tail skirts.

Undertrays are generally available in black or white, but can be supplied colour-matched to the bike at extra cost. The main material used in the construction of undertrays is ABS plastic, although fibreglass and carbon fibre options are also available.

Most undertrays have provision for mounting the indicators, reflector and licence plate, either direct to the undertray or via a mounting bracket.

There are a number of undertray styles available. Some accommodate the original rear light unit, whereas others have two or three lights fitted or use LED (Light Emitting Diode) rear lights.

Where an undertray is already fitted as standard equipment, further refinements can be made by fitting an aftermarket mounting for the indicators and licence plate. A 'tail tidy' will reduce the size of the rear end and smarten it up (see later in this chapter).

The fitting procedure will usually require the standard rear mudguard to be trimmed down and the bungee cord hooks to be removed. If you are likely to revert the bike back to standard in the future you might consider acquiring a second-hand rear mudguard from a breaker for this job.

Fitting an undertray

This procedure illustrates the fitting of a white undertray to match the bike's factory colour scheme. The original tail light fitment is retained.

4 Cut along the top edge of the mudguard using a hacksaw – make sure the wiring is not in the way!

1 Remove the front and rear seat pads, then remove the tail unit panels. If the seat lock is incorporated in the rear mudguard you will need to remove this too. For specific information refer to the workshop manual for your model.

5 When the mudguard is cut all the way round remove it from the bike.

2 Disconnect its wiring connector and undo the retaining nut to remove both indicators from the rear mudguard. Also remove the rear reflector.

6 Use a small cutting disc to get into the more restricted areas.

3 Use a piece of tape to mark the cutting line along the top edge of the mudguard on both sides of the bike.

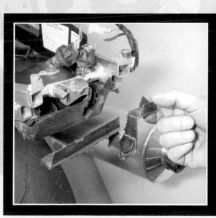

7 Remove the excess plastic from the rear of the mudguard.

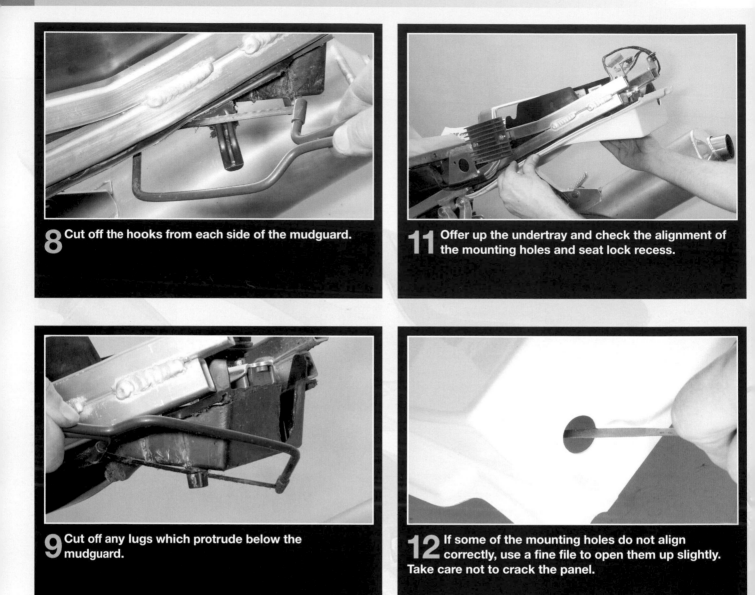

8 Cut off the hooks from each side of the mudguard.

11 Offer up the undertray and check the alignment of the mounting holes and seat lock recess.

9 Cut off any lugs which protrude below the mudguard.

12 If some of the mounting holes do not align correctly, use a fine file to open them up slightly. Take care not to crack the panel.

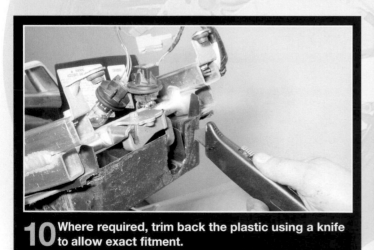

10 Where required, trim back the plastic using a knife to allow exact fitment.

13 With the undertray in position, refit the tail unit panels, seat lock and rear light.

14 You will need to remove the rear tail unit again to bolt the indicators to it. Mark the position of the indicators on the undertray; use a piece of masking tape to help prevent the drill from slipping.

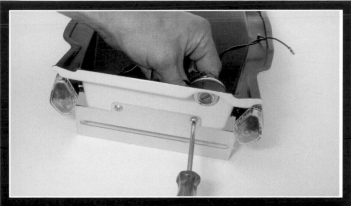

17 Remove the masking tape and screw the licence plate bracket to the undertray.

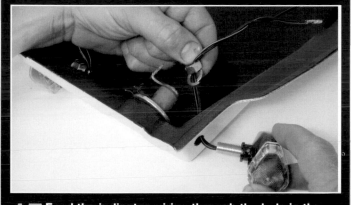

15 Feed the indicator wiring through the hole in the undertray and fit the nut and washer.

18 Refit the rear tail unit, then drill the holes for the licence plate light/reflector and fit it to the undertray.

16 Stick a piece of masking tape across the undertray. Align the licence plate bracket, then mark and drill the mounting hole positions.

19 The licence plate can now be fitted to the mounting bracket.

Tail Tidy

A tail tidy is essentially a mounting bracket which holds the indicators, reflector and licence plate, and will be a necessary fitment if you have modified the bike's rear end and dispensed with the standard rear mudguard. Most tail tidy brackets are of universal fitment.

Note that it is a legal requirement to fit a red reflector to the rear of the bike and for the licence plate to be illuminated with white light. In cases where the tail light lens does not also illuminate the licence light it will be necessary to obtain a mounting plate which has provision for a separate licence plate light.

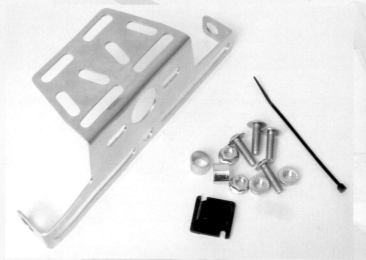

This bracket will accommodate the licence plate light, licence plate and indicators.

Adjustable brackets enable the indicator positions to be varied.

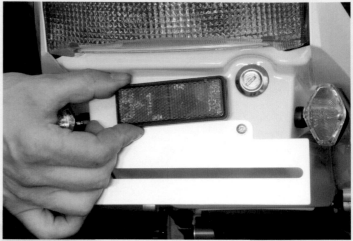

The reflector can be bolted or stuck to the undertray or tail tidy bracket.

A small white LED is a less conspicuous form of licence plate light, although you may need to fit a shield so that it doesn't shine a white light at the rear of the bike.

Licence plate

The legal size for a UK motorcycle licence plate is 228 x 178 mm (9 x 7 inches). The character size and spacing requirements are as follows and the registration must be displayed over two lines – single line plates are illegal.

Character height	64mm
Character width (except for figure No.1)	44mm
Character line width	10mm
Space between the characters	10mm
Upper, lower and side margins should be	11mm min
Space between the upper and lower rows of characters	13mm

Carbon fibre

Carbon fibre accessories range from yoke protectors, instrument surrounds, front mudguards, rear huggers, chainguards, air intakes and various mounting brackets and guards to the more exotic world of carbon fibre wheels, fairing panels and fuel tanks. As a material it is strong, lightweight and can easily be moulded into various shapes, although it is expensive to produce.

There are different styles of weave pattern, the two common ones being twill weave and plain weave. Depending on the construction, a carbon fibre component can be up to five times stronger than the equivalent component made from steel.

Carbon fibre is a composite material made up of several layers of carbon fibre texture, pre-impregnated with epoxy resins. During the production process the resin must be soft enough not to damage the delicate fibres whilst being able to function over a wide temperature range when hardened. Also the purpose of the epoxy resin is to bond the layers of carbon fibre and hold the weave in the correct position. The carbon fibre layers are placed into a mould in the shape of the final product, the mould is then cured in an oven and any air bubbles dispersed. The number of carbon layers required depends on the item application. The component is then coated with a clear varnish to give a high quality gloss finish.

Other materials can be incorporated in the production of carbon fibre components. Cost reductions can be made by incorporating a layer of glass fibre between the layers of carbon fibre as a filler. To give extra strength at certain stress points, layers of carbon Kevlar can be used between the layers of carbon fibre. These methods will give extra strength with only a slight weight increase.

Top quality wheels are often made of carbon fibre, such are the benefits of its strength and lightness. The weight saving over aluminium wheels is considerable even on composite wheels which use a mix of magnesium alloy and carbon fibre components.

Kevlar and aluminium coated fibre components use a similar manufacturing process to carbon fibre components. To identify the different materials, carbon fibre is black and silver, carbon Kevlar is yellow and black and, as you would expect, aluminium coated fibre is silver (see the "ghost hugger" illustrated).

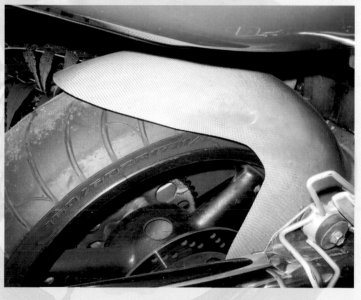

Carbon fibre items are usually supplied ready for fitting to the existing mountings and contain fixing kits where necessary. The holes in the panels are sometimes smaller than original equipment, so that it can be adjusted for a more secure fitment on the bike. The following procedures describe the fitting of several typical carbon components and there is reference to others, such as the carbon fibre engine guards, elsewhere in this book.

3 A strip of foam can also be stuck along the swingarm, where the hugger will seat.

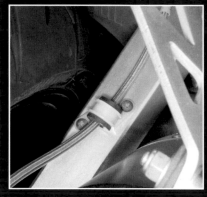

4 The rear brake hose mounting bracket secures the hugger in place on this model and will need to be removed beforehand.

Rear hugger fitting

1 Release its retaining bolts or clips and remove the original plastic chainguard.

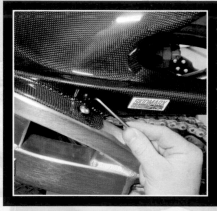

5 Install the hugger and tighten its mounting bolts; make sure the bolts are long enough to thread into the swingarm sufficiently.

2 On huggers which fit flat against the surface of the swingarm, a strip of foam (draught excluder) can be stuck to the underside of the hugger to make a good seal.

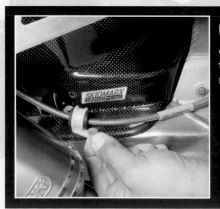

6 Secure the hugger on the other side of the swingarm with the brake hose mounting bracket.

Front mudguard fitting

The fixing method will vary depending on the arrangement of the brake lines and mudguard mounting points. Check the mounting bolt holes in the new mudguard – they may need to be enlarged slightly to accommodate the retaining bolts. If fitting new mounting bolts, make sure they are of the correct length – if too long they may foul the wheel or brake discs.

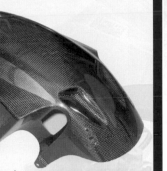

4 Brake line mounting brackets shown removed from the original mudguard.

1 Slacken and remove the mounting bolts from the original front mudguard.

5 Fit the brake line brackets to the carbon fibre mudguard and rivet them in place.

2 Unbolt the brake lines from the rear of the mudguard and withdraw it from the bike.

6 Fit the carbon fibre mudguard into place and tighten the mounting bolts.

3 Drill out the rivets in the original mudguard.

7 Secure the brake lines at both sides of the mudguard – note the use of P-clips.

Front sprocket cover fitting

The gearchange linkage rod may need to be removed for access on some models; refer to the workshop manual for further information.

1 Slacken the retaining bolts and remove the front sprocket cover.

2 Fit the carbon fibre cover in place and tighten the retaining bolts.

Frame guard fitting

Check the fitting instructions supplied with the frame guards. The Harris guards shown simply clip in place although other types may require sealant or have a screw fitting.

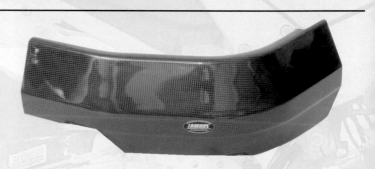

1 Undo the retaining screws and remove the fairing side panel.

2 Undo the retaining screws and unclip the inner trim panel from the air inlet duct.

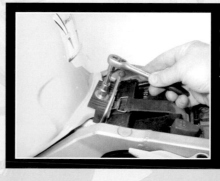

3 Remove the front seat pad and undo the rear mounting bolt from the fuel tank.

4 Lift the fuel tank slightly, then clip the carbon fibre guard into place along the side of the frame.

Body panels

Aftermarket bodywork is considerably cheaper than original equipment panels and is a viable alternative in the event of the fairing being damaged beyond repair. Replica replacement panels made from GRP (Glass Reinforced Plastic) or fibreglass are handmade and may vary slightly from factory panels. Other materials used in the manufacture of aftermarket bodywork are carbon fibre and carbon Kevlar, and although lighter, are much more expensive.

The panels are usually supplied in white and will require painting, whereas certain manufacturers may be able to colour match them to suit your requirements. Note that when fitting aftermarket panels, some trimming will usually be required.

Aftermarket front mudguard constructed from fibreglass.

Replica replacement bodywork

If fitting replica replacement bodywork for road bike use, the panels will need to accommodate the original headlights, indicators, air intakes, etc. The panels will be supplied pre-drilled, to attach to the original mounting points, although some adjustment of their position may be required to ensure perfect fitting.

Race or track day bodywork

If the bike is used for trackdays or racing a race fairing is the best option. It differs from replica bodywork in that it is not supplied with holes for the headlight, indicators, air intakes etc. and is generally made up of less panels to enable quick and easy removal and refitting.

Race panels are usually made from fibreglass and tend to be less expensive than replica bodywork. Mounting brackets, which would normally support lighting, instrumentation and mirrors on a road bike, are often changed for lighter items for racing purposes.

Dzus fairing panel fasteners are commonly used for race fairings – they are quick-release items for fast removal of the fairing panel. They are also known as D-clips and speed fasteners.

The lower section (belly pan) on race and track fairings does not have a drain hole in its base. This is intentional and ensures that if the engine blows and throws out any oil, it is retained in the belly pan and does not leak onto the track. If this type of fairing is fitted to a road bike, drill a hole in the base of the belly pan to allow rain water to drain. Failure to do so will cause rain water caught in the belly pan to spray out over the back wheel. If being used on a race track at a later date a rubber grommet can be used to block the hole.

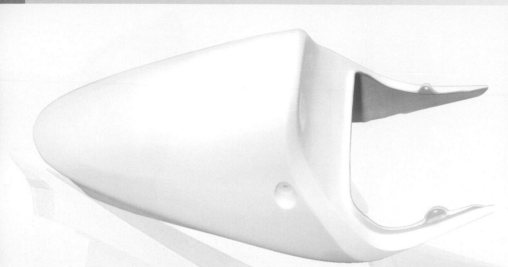

Single race seat unit

If considering a single seat unit, check whether the original seat pad can be used; on some seat units the seat area is filled in and an adhesive foam seat pad is stuck in its place. The foam seat pad might well be lighter and enable quick removal of the seat unit, but the original seat will be far more comfortable for road use.

For road use ensure that the race seat unit has the facility to fit a rear stop and tail light unit.

Huggers and mudguards

Huggers and mudguards are available in various colours and materials. Front mudguards are a direct replacement for the original units and use the same mounting points. Rear huggers are a bolt-on extra and will be supplied with a fitting kit. Whilst giving the rear of the bike a streamlined look, the hugger prevents water and dirt being sprayed over the rear suspension unit.

For more information on the fitting of front mudguards and huggers see the *Carbon fibre* section

The painted race seat unit should bolt straight onto the original rear sub-frame . . .

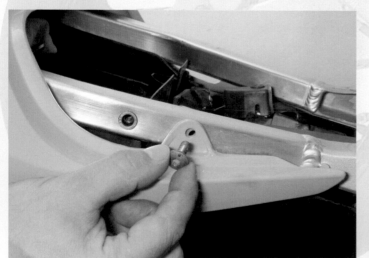

. . . and can be secured using the original bolts; slight adjustment of the mounting points may be necessary.

Most single seat units will accept an undertray.

Preparation for fitting

Check whether there are screws, clips, fasteners, etc. supplied with the aftermarket panels – you may need to purchase these separately.

Fit the fairing panels to the bike before having them painted. This will ensure they fit perfectly and avoid damaging the paintwork if trimming or drilling is required afterwards.

With the panels fitted, check they do not foul any components or restrict steering or suspension movement. For example, if the panels rest against the exhaust or any other hot component, overheating or fire could result. Carefully remove any sharp edges which might damage coolant pipes, brake lines or wiring. Note that panels which are already pre-drilled may need to have the holes opened out to make them fit neatly.

Plastic bodywork repair

Minor repairs to original equipment plastic body panels can be made using a kit. Most repair kits contain an adhesive mixture which bonds the cracked or broken panel and some can even reclaim stripped threads. Check the information on the packaging to ensure it is suitable for the type of repair you require – all kits contain full instructions.

Another repair method is plastic welding, although this does require skilled use of a hot air welding gun. High temperatures are required to heat the plastic welding rods and carry out the repair successfully. Body panels are made of various types of plastic (ABS, PP, PVC etc.) and each will require a compatible plastic welding rod – check the inside of the panel for such markings.

The procedure overleaf illustrates the repair of a cracked rear cowling using the Plastex kit. Whichever kit is used, follow the specific instructions provided.

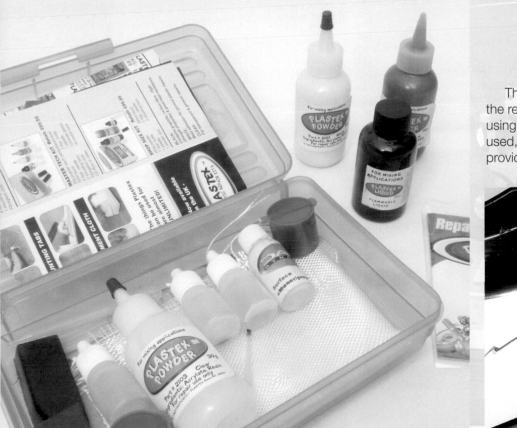

Stage 1 repair

Assess the type of repair required. For small stress-free cracks carry out the stage 1 repair. For a larger area of damage, particularly where the panel is under stress, carry out the stage 1 followed by the stage 2 procedures.

Always allow time for the repair to cure before refitting the panel to the bike.

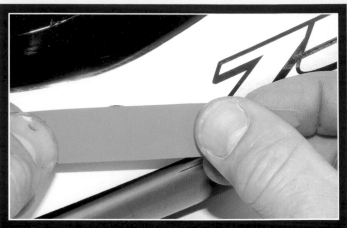

3 Turn the panel over and attach a piece of tape along the outside of the crack to prevent the Plastex mixture seeping through.

1 Working on the inside of the panel, clean the cracked area ready for the repair. Use a Dremel or small file to make a groove along the length of the crack.

4 Turn the panel back over and carefully pour the powder into the groove along the length of the crack. Mix the powder as described in the kit.

2 Wire brush along the damaged area, then wipe it with the cleaning fluid provided.

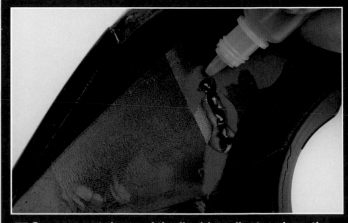

5 Squeeze out drops of the liquid applicator along the powder until it has all been covered.

Stage 2 repair

Where the panel is badly damaged or the crack is quite large with fragments missing, first carry out the Stage 1 procedure. When complete, carry out the Stage 2 procedure to reinforce the repair.

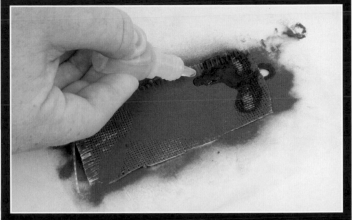

3 Using the liquid applicator, saturate the powder on the fibre cloth.

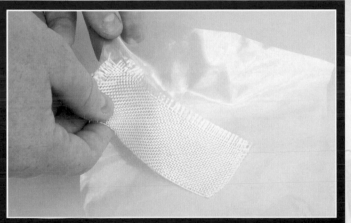

1 Cut a piece of the fibre reinforcement cloth provided to the size you require and lay the fibre cloth on a piece of plastic sheet. This sheet will be used to apply the cloth.

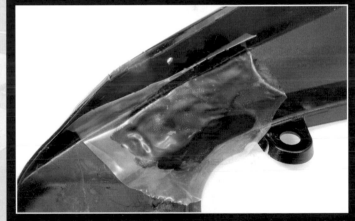

4 Pick up the plastic sheet with the fibre cloth attached and press it into place over the cracked area.

2 Pour the powder over the fibre cloth until the cloth is completely covered.

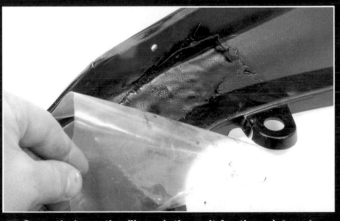

5 Smooth down the fibre cloth, wait for the mixture to cure, then peel the plastic sheet from the repair.

Decals

The application of decals, either additional to or instead of, the manufacturer's items, can give your bike an individual look. There are even companies who will supply decals created from your own design. Most decals have an adhesive backing and are very easy to fit.

Removing old decals

Standard original equipment decals are usually applied on top of bodywork lacquer and can be removed using heat. It will not be possible to use this technique where a lacquer has been applied to the panel on top of any decals; you can usually determine this by running your finger-nail over the decal edges. Do not attempt removal of the manufacturer's fuel tank decals.

Carefully heat up the transfer using a hot air gun, then peel it from the fairing. Be very careful not to hold the hot air gun too close to the fairing otherwise you might damage its surface – minimal heat is required to soften the adhesive.

After removing the transfers, use cleaning solvent to remove any remaining adhesive from the fairing panel.

Fitting new decals

This procedure illustrates the application of Motografix front upper fairing kit decals. The decals are supplied with a bonding adhesive on the rear of the pads and are ready for use when peeled off the backing sheet.

Fit the decals at room temperature and in perfectly dry conditions. If the decals are cold they will not fit to the contour of the fairing panel correctly.

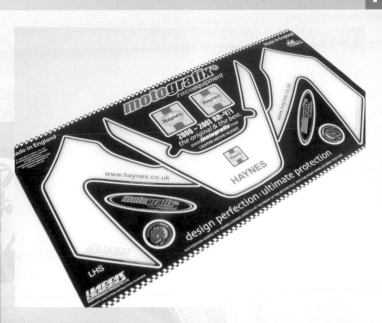

1 Wash the fairing panel to remove all traces of dust, dirt and grease. Dry the panel, then wipe the area using methylated spirit or similar.

2 Remove the decal from the backing sheet.

3 Align the decal on the fairing panel and press it firmly into place.

For a race bike look, manufacturers' logos can be fitted along the lower belly pan. Remove existing decals from the belly pan, then wash and dry the area thoroughly as described above. Lay out the decals on a worktop to establish their best position.

1 Peel the backing paper off and fit the first decal in place.

2 Work your way along the belly pan, keeping the decals in line and evenly spaced. Use a clean cloth to smooth down the decals.

Bolt kits and Bling

Bolts, nuts, screws, reservoir caps and paddock stand bobbins are just some of the items available in colour-anodised finishes. These are mainly produced from aluminium, with stainless or titanium items for certain, more critical, applications.

Maintaining a colour theme throughout the bike can transform its appearance, whereas the use of stainless steel bolts has the added benefit of being corrosion resistant. Titanium bolts should be used in high stress areas, such as for the brake system, engine mountings, suspension and steering – never use alloy bolts for these components.

Aluminium

Aluminium fasteners and accessories are lightweight and produced in a wide range of colours. Suitable stress-free applications are for securing fairing panels, screens, huggers, fuel caps, light units, heel plates etc. If you are in any doubt about the suitability of the bolts, check with the manufacturer.

When replacing engine casing bolts, always check the length of the bolts as they are removed. Some bolts are longer than others.

Always use copper-grease on the threads of fasteners to prevent corrosion.

Fork pre-load adjusters are held in place by grub screws and enable easy adjustment of the pre-load setting. Check that the adjusters do not foul on the surrounding components, such as the steering damper rod, by moving the steering from side to side.

Brake fluid reservoir caps are available for the front and rear brake fluid reservoirs and for clutch fluid reservoir. Their fitting will be model-specific.

Some caps are available with a logo etched into their surface, such as this polished brake fluid reservoir cap.

Fairing panel fastener kits are model-specific. Make note of the screw lengths as you remove the original fasteners.

Titanium

Titanium is widely used in racing, not only because it is equally as strong as steel, but because it is 40% lighter. The torque values for titanium bolts are the same as for steel bolts, but take care to use the exact fitting spanner, socket or Allen key when tightening them - if the tool slips the titanium head is likely to be damaged. Always use copper grease to lightly coat fastener threads.

Replacement oil filler caps should include an O-ring seal. Thread diameter and pitch will vary between models, so make sure the cap suits your bike.

Aluminium colour-anodised sprocket nuts with stainless thread inserts to suit their high-stress application.

Many replacement oil filler caps are pre-drilled to allow them to be lock-wired, which is a requirement for racing.

Colour-anodised cable adjusters are very high viz.

Titanium disc bolts are supplied as a kit and available in a range of colours.

A selection of paddock stand bobbins. Refer to Chapter 10 for details of crash protector bobbins.

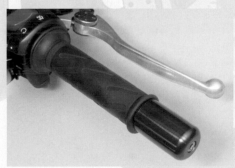

Bar end weights are produced in a variety of colours.

Apply copper grease to the threads.

Track Days

All that performance and nowhere to use it – or is there ?

As our roads become ever more congested and speed cameras pop up on every road worth riding, it is more difficult to enjoy ride-outs on a nice sunny evening or weekend. As well as this you also have to watch out for pot-holes, diesel spills on roundabouts and car drivers. The answer is "Track Days".

You have probably talked about it – I know I have – and never done anything about it. There is always an excuse – I don't know what to do or where to go? How much is it going to cost, is my bike suitable, and most of all, am I going to look a fool in front of all the other riders?

Firstly get in touch with the circuit of your choice and find out when they are running bike track days. You can then either book over the phone, ask them to send you a booking form or book on line. The website trackdays.co.uk has information on all circuits, including dates and cost, also a map and the length of the circuit.

If you live close enough to a circuit, it may help to attend a track day first as a spectator. Always check with the circuit beforehand to make sure this will be OK; most circuits will allow this (at no cost) as long as you stick to the spectator areas, for safety reasons. This will give you chance to look around and talk to some of the riders, familiarise yourself with the set-up and how the day is run.

When booking, always state if it is your first time on a track. It does not matter whether you have been riding for three years or thirty years; if you have never ridden on a track before then always begin as a novice. Most tracks usually run three groups: novice, intermediate and advance.

Some circuits run a "New to Track" group, where in the opening session, the circuit instructors spend time explaining and demonstrating the correct lines to take around the circuit. Ask about this when booking.

There could be 30 riders or more out on the track in each session. If it is your first time, it might be less daunting to go when there are less riders out at a time, so check beforehand. For example, the Castle Combe circuit featured in the photographs only allows 12 riders (+ instructors) out in each group session.

Always check the rules and regulations for the circuit you will be attending, these are available on request.

Preparation

Protective wear

Helmets must be to the ACU, FIM or MCRCB required specification. They should have the ACU official stamp or comply with BSI 6658 or ECE Regulation 2205. The use of earplugs is recommended.

Leathers must be full one-piece or two-piece zip together (all the way round 360° construction). No titanium "sparkies" knee sliders are allowed. The use of back protectors is recommended.

Gloves and boots must be of a leather construction, with no metal studs. No titanium "sparkies" toe sliders are allowed.

CAUTION

While out on the track, do not carry mobile phones or keys in your pockets because if you have a spill these could cause serious injury. Also remove watches, especially those with metal straps.

Bike preparation

It is the rider's responsibility to ensure that the bike is safe to use on a race circuit. Don't leave it until the day before to check your bike over, always prepare it a week in advance.

Check your bike for any leaks or loose components. Pay particular attention to the tyres, chain and

sprockets and fluid levels. You may need to tape up the mirrors or lights when you get to the circuit, so take some masking tape along just in case. Don't turn up with a noisy exhaust, they will not let you out on the track; the recommended noise level at most circuits is 105dB, which means you need to use the standard exhaust.

Make sure there's plenty of life in the tyres – the sides are going to take the most wear. Remember that when the day is over, you have to ride the bike home so you will need some tread left! If you have the luxury of a van or trailer to take your bike to the circuit, then this may be an option you should consider.

Consider fitting crash protectors – if the bike is dropped they could save you a lot of money. If you do drop the bike you may break a lever (gear, clutch, brake) or a footpeg and if this happens after only two laps, then that's the end of your track day. Regular track day users often carry spare levers and footpegs for this reason and there's often someone selling a varied assortment of tools and spares at the circuit. As a last resort, if the bike is damaged and cannot be ridden home, most circuits will store your bike for a mutually agreed period.

Some circuits allow video cameras, but they have to be mounted securely on the bike using the correct mounting brackets. Check with the circuit you are attending before fitting one.

Your insurance policy will probably not cover track days. Insurance cover is not required to participate in a track day, but it is advisable to arrange additional cover for the day. Check with your insurance company and they will be able to advise on cost.

Most circuits will allow you to take someone with you, as long as they stay within the spectator area and follow instructions from marshals and staff members.

Most tracks are open for use at 9.00am, so you will need to get to the circuit for about 7.30am. This will allow time for signing on, noise check and briefing, so give yourself plenty of time.

Make sure you have enough fuel for the morning sessions; e.g. if you do three sessions in the morning at 10 laps a session, on a 2 mile circuit, then you are going to cover 60 miles. Note that you will be getting less miles to the gallon on the circuit than you would under normal circumstances on the road, so remember to allow for this. Some circuits have fuel facilities.

The lunch break is normally from 12:30 to 13:30, which gives you plenty of time to have something to eat (avoid heavy meals) and to re-fuel. Most circuits will have catering facilities and serve hot and cold food throughout the day. Drink water between sessions to avoid dehydration and thus maintain your concentration.

WARNING

No lap timing or data logging equipment is allowed at track days, this is not a race day!

Programme

Signing on

The first thing to do is sign on, you will need to show your driving licence. Look for signs to the reception or clubhouse and get signed in.

Noise Check

Exhaust noise is measured at a distance of half a metre from the exhaust outlet using the instrument shown. The throttle is held open at three quarters maximum revs for the test, so if your bike red lines at 12,000 rpm you will need to hold the throttle open at 9000 rpm for a short time. It should read less than 105dB, otherwise you will not be allowed out on the track. You can go away and see if you can make it quieter, but depending on the circuit, you might not be able to get a refund if it is too loud. If you are running a standard exhaust system, then this should not

be a problem. Some circuits have a 98dB noise limit: this is not a static check, it is checked on a drive by.

Briefing

Make sure you attend the briefing. If you turn up late, report to a member of the organising party who will then make arrangements for you to have an individual briefing. This is probably the most important part of the day; listen to what is said and it should help the day go smoothly without any problems. Safety is always top priority at any circuit; if at the end of the briefing you are not sure about something, ask. During the briefing session you will be shown the racing line around the circuit, and the relevant braking and turning points plus the apex of corners.

Check which group you are in. If you

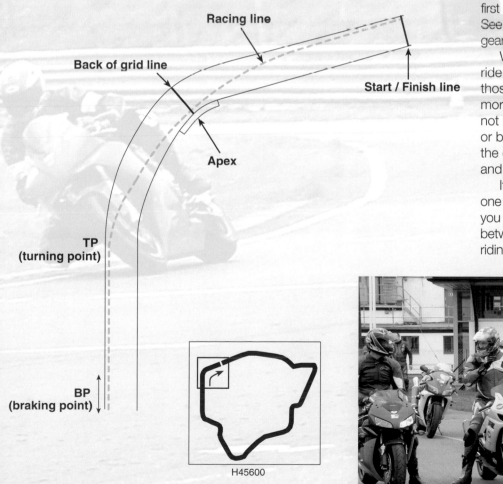

Racing line

Back of grid line

Start / Finish line

Apex

TP
(turning point)

BP
(braking point)

H45600

are not going out immediately, watch the first group and see what the procedure is. See what lines they take and listen to the gearchange in and out of the corners.

When you get out on track, always ride within your capabilities and not those of the rider in front, who may be more experienced than you. It does not matter whether you are at the front or back of the group – at the end of the day it will be a fantastic experience and a SAFE one.

If you experience any problems, see one of the instructors and they will give you advice. There is always time between track sessions to discuss your riding skills (or lack of) with the instructor.

Always read the signs around the circuit – they are there for your safety. This circuit consists mainly of right-hand corners so the left side of the tyre is not going to warm up as quickly as the right.

At this circuit, there is a traffic light sequence for going out on track, red for stop and green for go. Below the lights is a number board showing which group is waiting to go out.

⚠️ *Always be aware of the flags – they are there for your safety*

Yellow	Slow down (checking mirrors), do not overtake
Red	Slow down (checking mirrors), return to pit lane, no overtaking, session has been stopped
Blue	Allow faster bikes to pass
Black	Return to the pits immediately and report to a marshal or instructor
Chequered	End of session, reduce speed and return to pit lane

SAFETY

- **No wheelies, stoppies or riding dangerously or you will be removed from the circuit**
- **Medical services are always present at track days, there will be an ambulance with paramedics and a doctor**

If you would like a picture to prove your skills around a race track, you will find that most circuits have a resident photographer. The photographer will usually go out in the morning session and take a selection of photographs and at lunchtime you can view these to see if there is one you wish to purchase.

If you encounter any problems during the day, see the circuit manager or instructors, they are there to help you.

WARNING

Remember when leaving any circuit, you have left the track, so ride carefully and within the speed limits. The police know when these track days are run and will often have speed camera patrols in the area. Keep the speeding for the track, it's a lot safer.

Crash protectors

Crash protectors are excellent value for money and will greatly reduce damage to the bike in the event of a spill. Although included here in the Track Day chapter, the fitting of crash protectors makes good sense for all bike use. Probably the most common causes of bike damage are the bike falling over during slow speed manoeuvres and dropping the bike on sharp corners or roundabouts.

Crash protectors are manufactured from solid white or black high density nylon and mounted with high tensile steel bolts. The mounting bolt length is important to ensure a secure mounting so check that the items purchased are recommended for your bike. This is particularly important where the mounting point threads into the engine block.

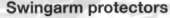

Swingarm protectors

Known as swingarm bobbins or cotton reels, these items protect the swingarm and also enable the use of a paddock stand. Many bikes have threads located in the swingarm to accommodate paddock stand bobbins and the swingarm protectors can simply be fitted in their place.

This fairing panel was not marked at all when the bike was dropped. The only damage was a scuff to the end of the crash protector and a dent in the rider's ego.

1 Thread the swingarm protector into the paddock stand bobbin mounting threads.

2 Using an Allen key, tighten the swingarm protector bolt.

Exhaust protectors

Exhaust protectors cover the leading edge of the can and also provide a form of heat shield. They are retained with an adjustable fixing strap, suitable for 4.5 to 5.5 inch diameter cans, and are available in three finishes: carbon fibre look, gloss silver and black. A strip of silicone rubber underneath the fixing strap protects the exhaust can.

Always check that no components will be fouled by the fitting of the exhaust protector and that it doesn't interfere with suspension and swingarm movement.

2 Slide the protector around the can so that the rubber strip can be cut to the correct length.

1 Slacken the fixing strap and place the exhaust can protector with the rubber strip on the exhaust can.

3 Position the protector in its correct position and tighten the fixing strap securely. Make sure the rubber strip locates between the fixing strap and the exhaust can.

Bar end protectors

Bar end protectors are specially machined steel bar-end weights with renewable high-density nylon ends.

1 Slacken the retaining screw and remove the original bar end weight.

2 Use thread lock when fitting the bar end weight screw. Check on the right-hand side that the throttle grip is free to rotate – it must snap shut when released.

Bike/frame protectors

The bike/frame crash protectors must be able to take the weight of the bike on impact and as such it is important to purchase high quality items. Depending on the manufacturer, they are known as fairing protectors, crash mushrooms, crash sliders or crash bungs.

Most protectors mount to the point at which the engine and frame meet, this being considered the strongest point on the machine. Do not be tempted to mount them at other, less rigid, points on the bike. In some cases the fairing side panels will need to be drilled to accommodate the crash protectors at the appropriate point.

NOTE

The fitting procedure will vary from model to model. Follow the specific instructions supplied in the kit, particularly the positioning of any spacers provided.

1 Remove the top bolt from the right-hand engine mounting bracket (as you are sitting on the bike).

3 Tighten the crash protector mounting bolt to the manufacturer's torque setting for the engine mounting bracket. Make sure a washer is fitted between the head of the bolt and the crash protector.

2 Fit the crash protector to the engine mounting bracket, making sure the 3mm alloy spacer is fitted between the crash protector and the engine mounting bracket.

4 Note that the mounting arrangement may differ for each side. In this case a 12mm alloy spacer was required between the crash protector and the engine mounting bracket on the left side.

Fork protectors

The mounting kit fits through the hollow front wheel axle bolt and secures a nylon protector on each side of the wheel. Fork protectors shield the lower part of the fork legs and brake calipers from damage.

1 Slacken and remove the original axle bolt from the right-hand side of the front wheel (as you are sitting on the bike).

4 Slide one of the nylon fork protectors onto the bar, then slide the bar through the axle bolt and axle shaft. Note that the protectors are usually handed so check that you've installed them accordingly.

2 Fit the new axle bolt from the fitting kit and torque it to the manufacturer's specified figure.

5 Working at the left-hand side of the wheel, slide the other fork protector over the end of the threaded bar and fit the washer and nyloc nut.

3 Fit the nyloc nut and washer to one end of the bar supplied in the kit and run the nyloc nut on the bar until a couple of threads are showing.

6 Tighten the nyloc nuts so that the bar protrudes an equal distance on both sides. Do not over-tighten the nyloc nuts.

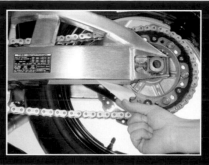

1 Stick a length of masking tape on the swingarm where the toe guard will be positioned. This will make it easier to mark out the position.

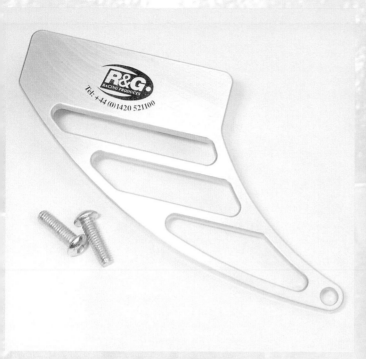

2 Locate the toe guard on the underside of the swingarm and mark the position of its two mounting holes on the masking tape.

Toe guards

The toe guard fits under the swingarm and prevents the rider's foot contacting the chain and rear sprocket in the event of a spill. It is also known as a "shark fin" or chainguard. The fitting of a toe guard is compulsory on race bikes and similar legislation may follow for track day use.

3 Drill two 5mm holes in the positions marked. Note that the masking tape will also help prevent the drill sliding about on the shiny surface.

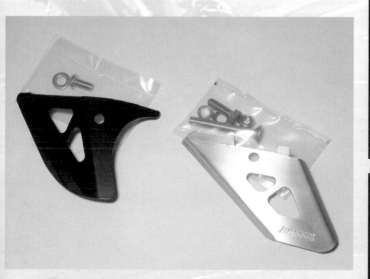

4 Using a suitably sized tap, thread the holes in the swingarm to suit an M6 Allen screw.

Toe guards are available in different styles and materials. Most are universal fitting and can be bolted, screwed or riveted to the swingarm.

5 Apply thread locking compound to the threads of the two M6 x 20mm Allen key screws from the fitting kit and fit the toe guard to the swingarm.

Engine casings

If your bike is knocked off its stand or it takes a slide down the road, the alternator and clutch engine casings are likely to sustain a degree of damage. Usually only surface scoring will be evident, but a hard knock could fracture or smash the casing with resultant oil loss. Replacement heavy duty casings provide a greater degree of protection than standard casings. Alternatively there's the less expensive option of fitting an engine guard.

Heavy duty casings

The fitting of heavy duty engine casings is recommended for racing or regular track day use. Ensure that the replacement casing is suitable for your model of bike and always fit a new gasket. Note that it will be necessary to drain the engine oil before fitting the clutch casing.

Some heavy duty covers are fitted with a renewable skid pad on the lower part of the cover, made of stainless steel or high density nylon.

Carbon fibre engine guard

The most inexpensive form of engine casing protection is the pre-shaped carbon fibre engine guard. These guards are highly durable, lightweight and bond to the bike's original engine casing like a second skin. The silicone fixing remains in a "rubbery" state when cured, so as to help absorb the initial force on any impact.

NOTE

Allow at least 24 hours for the adhesive to cure before using the bike. If the temperature is less than 20°C, then allow a little longer for the adhesive to cure.

2 Wash down the engine casings and the inside of the carbon fibre engine guard with soapy water. Using a lint free cloth dry the casing and engine guard to remove any residue from the soapy water.

3 Apply a thin coat (2 to 4mm) of the adhesive to the engine casing. Do not apply any adhesive to the outer edge as this will cause excess adhesive to squeeze out.

1 Remove the fairing panel to enable full access to the engine casing.

4 Make sure the guard is positioned correctly and press it into place over the engine casing. Any excess adhesive will need to be cleaned away immediately using white spirit.

Reference

Tools

Tech Terms

Index

Thanks to:

Tools

The fitting of most aftermarket components will necessitate an assortment of tools, although nothing too specialised. As a rule it is better to buy the more expensive, good quality tools; cheaper tools are likely to wear out faster and need to be renewed more often.

The following list of tools will serve as a basic toolkit. In addition, items such as an electric drill, hacksaw, files, soldering iron and a workbench equipped with a vice, may be required. A stock of bolts, screws, nuts and washers is also useful to have at hand.

WARNING

Always aim to purchase tools which meet the relevant safety standards, this is to avoid the risk of a poor quality tool breaking while being used, causing injury to yourself or damage to the component being worked on.

Spanners

A good range of spanner sizes is required to cover all fasteners on the bike, say from 8 to 22 mm. A set of combination spanners are the most useful, having an open end and a ring end. When removing some nuts and through-bolts you will often need two spanners of the same size, so it is best to have two sets of spanners.

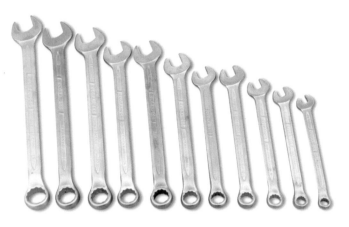

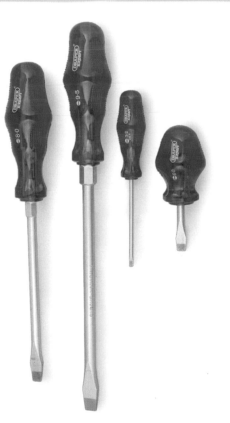

Breaker bar

A good quality breaker bar will enable extra leverage to be applied for **undoing** very tight retaining bolts. Use a torque wrench for refitting the bolts, so that the fastener can be secured to the correct torque loading.

Screwdrivers

There are different types of screwdrivers available, the most common being Pozi, Torx or flat-bladed screwdrivers. Always buy good quality screwdrivers, as their ends can easily be damaged.

Ratchet and socket set

Socket sets are available in three drive sizes: 1/4, 3/8, and 1/2 inch. For chassis components a 1/2 inch drive set will be required, whereas a 1/4 inch set is ideal for work on delicate components.

Torque wrench

Essential when refitting suspension, steering, engine and brake system components to ensure that their bolts/nuts are tightened correctly. Refer to the workshop manual for your bike for torque setting values.

Allen keys

Many fasteners are of the Allen head type, particularly those used for fairing panels. Allen-head bolts used to secure suspension, steering, engine and brake components will require Allen bits which can be used in a socket rather than Allen keys; this is because they are tightened to a high torque setting. A set of T-bar Allen keys is useful because they have a long reach and allow a quicker action than Allen keys; they are however difficult to use where space is restricted.

C-spanner

Used for adjusting the rear shock absorber pre-load ring and the steering head bearing adjuster ring. C-spanners are available in different sizes and some are adjustable.

Pliers

A selection of pliers will be needed for various jobs on the bike.

Hammer

There are several variations of the conventional hammer, including rubber, hide and plastic head types for specific purposes. Select the correct type for the job in hand – many components on a motorcycle are fragile and easily broken.

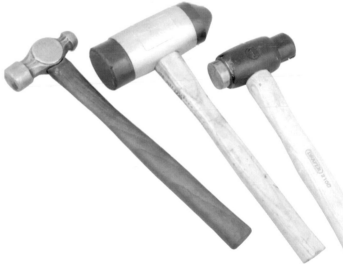

Self gripping pliers

Also known as vice grips or Mole grips, these are very useful as they can be altered to fit different sizes. When the correct size has been set the grips are locked in position and do not require hand pressure to grip the fastener. These are also available as a long nose version to get into awkward places.

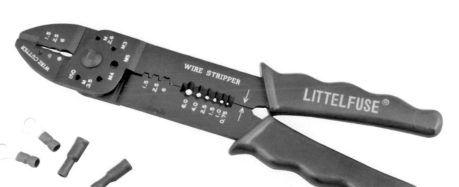

Wire cutters and crimping pliers

A good pair of wire cutters and a crimping tool will be needed for the fitting of electrical components, such as alarms or digital gear indicators. A soldering iron may also be needed.

Tech Terms

ABS Acrylonitrile butadiene styrene. A type of thermoplastic.

ABS (Anti-lock braking system) A system, usually electronically controlled, that senses incipient wheel lockup during braking and relieves hydraulic pressure at the wheel which is about to skid.

Aftermarket Components designed for the motorcycle but not by the motorcycle manufacturer. Compare with OE (Original Equipment).

Air filter Paper or foam element for trapping dirt and dust particles in the engine's air intake system.

Allen key A hexagonal wrench which fits into a recessed hexagonal hole in a fastener.

Anti-seize compound A coating that reduces the risk of seizing on fasteners that are subjected to high temperatures, such as exhaust clamp bolts and nuts, e.g. copper-based grease.

Axle A shaft on which a wheel revolves. Also known as a spindle.

BHP Brake Horsepower. The British measurement for engine power output. Power output is now usually expressed in kilowatts (kW).

Bleeding The process of removing air from an hydraulic system via a bleed valve.

Braided hoses Hydraulic hoses re-enforced with stainless steel braiding.

Brake disc The component of a disc brake that rotates with the wheel.

Brake pads The friction material which contacts the brake disc when the brake is applied.

Burr Rough edge left on a component after machining or as a result of excessive wear.

Caliper The non-rotating part of a disc brake that straddles the disc and carries the brake pads. A caliper is also a measuring device that can be set to measure inside or outside diameters of an object.

Carbon fibre This is a composite material made up of several layers of carbon fibre texture, which is pre-impregnated with epoxy resins.

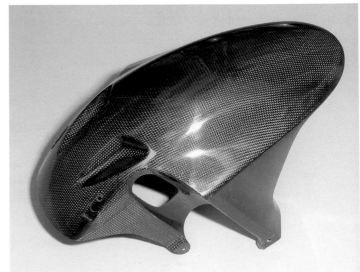

Carburettor Device for mixing fuel and air in the correct proportions and controlling engine speed.

Circlip A ring-shaped clip used to prevent endwise movement of cylindrical parts and shafts. An internal circlip is installed in a groove in a housing; an external circlip fits into a groove on the outside of a cylindrical piece such as a shaft. Also known as a snap-ring.

Clearance The amount of space between two parts. For example, between a piston and a cylinder, between a bearing and a journal, etc.

Clip-ons Separate handlebar units which clamp around the front forks, either under or over the top yoke.

Clutch The device used to disengage the engine from the gearbox to permit gearchanging. Most motorcycles use wet multi-plate clutches.

CNC (Computer numerical control) A method of component manufacture in which the component is cut from a solid billet of material.

Coil spring A spiral of elastic steel found in various sizes throughout a vehicle, for example as a springing medium in the suspension and in the valve train.

Compression Reduction in volume, and increase in pressure and temperature, of a gas, caused by squeezing it into a smaller space.

Compression damping Controls the speed the suspension compresses when hitting a bump.

Crash protectors High density nylon extensions fitted to the bike extremities to minimise damage in the event of a crash.

Diaphragm spring A single sprung plate often used in clutches.

Double-overhead camshaft (DOHC) An engine that uses two overhead camshafts, one for the intake valves and one for the exhaust valves.

Dynamometer Specialist test station for measuring the bikes power and torque output.

Dynojet kit A set of carburettor jets, needles and sometimes springs to replace the standard original equipment items.

Earth return The return path of an electrical circuit, utilising the motorcycle's frame.

ECU (Electronic Control Unit) A computer which controls the engine's ignition and fuelling systems.

Endless chain A chain having no joining link. Common use for cam chains and final drive chains.

Exhaust baffle Removal baffle pipe set in the end of the exhaust can.

Exhaust can Detachable silencer either bolted or clamped to the exhaust link pipe.

Flooding Term used to describe a high fuel level in the carburettor float chambers, leading to fuel overflow. Also refers to excess fuel in the combustion chamber due to incorrect starting technique.

Forged A method of manufacture where the component is pressed into shape.

Free length The no-load state of a component when measured. Clutch, valve and fork spring lengths are measured at rest, without any preload.

Freeplay The amount of travel before any action takes place. The looseness in a linkage, or an assembly of parts, between the initial application of force and actual movement. For example, the distance the rear brake pedal moves before the rear brake is actuated.

Fuel injection The fuel/air mixture is metered electronically and directed into the engine intake ports (indirect injection) or into the cylinders (direct injection). Sensors supply information on engine speed and conditions.

Fuel/air mixture The charge of fuel and air going into the engine. See **Stoichiometric ratio**.

Fuse An electrical device which protects a circuit against accidental overload. The typical fuse contains a soft piece of metal which is calibrated to melt at a predetermined current flow (expressed as amps) and break the circuit.

Gear indicator Electronic device mounted on the instruments to display the current gear position.

Gear ratio Comparison of gear rotation according to the number of teeth.

Heel guard Plate fixed to the rider's footpeg assembly to prevent contact with the rear wheel or chain.

HT (High Tension) Description of the electrical circuit from the secondary winding of the ignition coil to the spark plug.

Hugger Close-fitting rear wheel mudguard, often incorporating the chainguard.

Hydraulic A liquid filled system used to transmit pressure from one component to another. Common uses on motorcycles are brakes and clutches.

Hygroscopic Water absorbing. In motorcycle applications, braking efficiency will be reduced if glycol-based hydraulic fluid absorbs water from the air – care must be taken to keep new brake fluid in tightly sealed containers.

lbf ft Pounds-force feet. An imperial unit of torque. Sometimes written as ft-lbs.

lbf in Pound-force inch. An imperial unit of torque, applied to components where a very low torque is required. Sometimes written as in-lbs.

Ignition advance Means of increasing the timing of the spark at higher engine speeds. Done electronically by the engine's ECU..

Ignition timing The moment at which the spark plugs fire, expressed in the number of crankshaft degrees before the piston reaches the top of its stroke, or in the number of millimetres before the piston reaches the top of its stroke.

Infinity (∞) Description of an open-circuit electrical state, where no continuity exists.

Inverted forks (upside down forks) The sliders or lower legs are held in the yokes and the fork tubes or stanchions are connected to the wheel axle. Less unsprung weight and stiffer construction than conventional forks.

Jack-up plates A pair of plates which alters the position of the rider's footpegs. It is also used as a term for a pair of suspension linkage plates for adjusting the height of the rear suspension.

Kevlar A composite material made up of several layers of Kevlar fibre texture. Five times stronger than steel.

LCD Abbreviation for Liquid Crystal Display.

LDPE (PE-LD) Low density polyethylene. A type of thermoplastic.

LED Abbreviation for Light Emitting Diode.

LLDPE (PE-LLD) Linear low density polyethylene. A type of thermoplastic.

Locknut A nut used to lock an adjustment screw or nut, or other threaded component, in place.

Lockstops The lugs on the lower clamp (yoke) which abut those on the frame, preventing handlebar-to-fuel tank contact.

LT (Low Tension) The electrical circuit from the power supply to the primary winding of the ignition coil.

Maintenance-free (MF) battery A sealed battery which does not require topping up.

Master cylinder Device for compressing the hydraulic fluid in proportion to the leverage applied at the brake/clutch lever or brake pedal.

MDPE (PE-MD) Medium density polyethylene. A type of thermoplastic.

Monoshock A single suspension unit linking the swingarm or suspension linkage to the frame.

Multigrade oil Having a wide viscosity range (e.g. 10W40). The W stands for Winter, thus the viscosity ranges from SAE10 when cold to SAE40 when hot.

Multimeter An electrical test instrument with the capability to measure voltage, current and resistance. Some meters also incorporate a continuity tester and buzzer.

Nm Newton metres. A metric unit of torque.

NOx Oxides of Nitrogen. A common toxic pollutant emitted by petrol engines at higher temperatures.

Octane The measure of a fuel's resistance to knock.

OE (Original Equipment) Relates to components fitted to a motorcycle as standard or replacement parts supplied by the motorcycle manufacturer.

Ohm The unit of electrical resistance. Ohms = Volts ÷ Current.

Ohmmeter An instrument for measuring electrical resistance.

Oil cooler System for diverting engine oil outside of the engine to a radiator for cooling purposes.

Open-circuit An electrical condition where there is a break in the flow of electricity – no continuity (high resistance).

Organic A term used by brake pads manufacturers to describe non-asbestos pads.

O-ring A type of sealing ring made of a special rubber-like material; in use, the O-ring is compressed into a groove to provide a seal.

Oxidization To undergo a chemical reaction with oxygen, as in rusting.

PA Polyamide (Nylon). A thermoplastic with different types available. PA6, PA11, PA12 and PA66.

PBT Polybutylene terephthalate. A type of thermoplastic.

Polarity Either negative or positive earth (ground), determined by which battery lead is connected to the frame (earth return). Modern motorcycles are negative earth.

Power Commander Electronic device for optimising ignition and fuelling requirements. Can be programmed.

PP (PPN) Polypropylene. A type of thermoplastic.

PPC Polypropylene copolymer. A type of thermoplastic.

PPH Polypropylene homopolymer. A type of thermoplastic.

Pre-ignition A condition where the fuel/air mixture ignites before the spark plug fires. Often due to a hot spot in the combustion chamber caused by carbon build-up. Engine has a tendency to 'run-on'.

Pre-load (suspension) The amount a spring is compressed when in the unloaded state. Preload can be applied by gas, spacer or mechanical adjuster.

PS Pfedestärke – a German interpretation of BHP.

PSI Pounds-force per square inch. Imperial unit of pressure.

PTFE Polytetrafluroethylene. A type of thermoplastic which has a low friction substance.

PVC Polyvinyl chloride. A type of thermoplastic.

Quartz halogen bulb Tungsten filament surrounded by a halogen gas. Typically used for the headlight.

Radial master cylinder Race type master cylinder where the operating lever is perpendicular to the piston.

Radial play Up and down movement about a shaft.

Radial ply tyres Tyre plies run across the tyre (from bead to bead) and around the circumference of the tyre. Less resistant to tread distortion than other tyre types.

Rake A feature of steering geometry – the angle of the steering head in relation to the vertical.

Rear sets Aftermarket footpegs assemblies which position the control higher and rear of the original OE components.

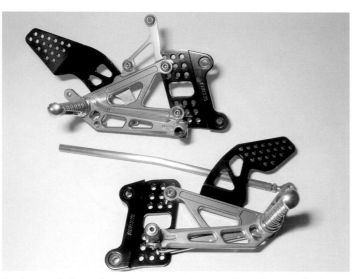

Rebound damping A means of controlling the oscillation of a suspension unit spring after it has been compressed. Resists the spring's natural tendency to bounce back after being compressed.

Resistance Electrical resistance is measured in ohms. An electrical component's ability to pass electrical current.

Re-valving Aftermarket kit for improving the front fork or rear shock damping cartridge.

Rev light Programmable electronic instrument triggered by the bike's tacho to display engine speed in terms of a series of lights.

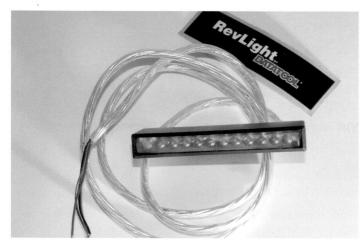

RON (Research Octane Number) A measure of a fuel's resistance to knock.

Rotor A shaped ignition rotor with raised triggers bolted to the end of the crankshaft. Also that part of an alternator which rotates inside the stator.

rpm revolutions per minute.

Runout The amount of wobble (in-and-out movement) of a wheel or shaft as it's rotated. The amount a shaft rotates `out-of-true'. The out-of-round condition of a rotating part.

SAE (Society of Automotive Engineers) A standard for the viscosity of a fluid.

Sag In terms of suspension, sag is the amount a spring compress from its unladen state (wheels off the ground) to with the rider seated.

Sealant A liquid or paste used to prevent leakage at a joint. Sometimes used in conjunction with a gasket.

Short-circuit An electrical condition where current shorts to earth (ground), bypassing the circuit components.

Sintered Brake pad material made up of a number of particles (including metal) compressed together.

Slipper clutch Device which enables the clutch to automatically disengage under conditions where road speed is greater than engine speed.

Sprocket A toothed wheel shaped to engage a chain or belt. Commonly used on motorcycle final drives and camshaft drives.

Stanchion The inner sliding part of the front forks, held by the yokes. Often called a fork tube.

Steering damper Hydraulic device for damping the steering movement from side-to-side.

Steering head Moveable joint between the motorcycle's frame and front end. Consists of the frame headstock and steering stem and yokes.

Stoichiometric ratio The optimum chemical air/fuel ratio for a petrol engine, said to be 14.7 parts of air to 1 part of fuel.

Swingarm Moveable joint between the motorcycle's frame and rear end. Supports the rear wheel and rear suspension.

Tail tidy Special bracket for mounting the licence plate and rear indicators to the undertray.

Tank pad Plastic or carbon pad which protects the tank's paintwork being scratched from contact with the rider's jacket buckles and zips.

Teflon Trademark name for PTFE (Polytetrafluroethylene).

TCS Traction Control System. An electronically-controlled system which senses wheel spin and reduces engine speed accordingly.

TDC Top Dead Centre denotes that the piston is at its highest point in the cylinder.

Thread-locking compound Solution applied to fastener threads to prevent slackening. Select type to suit application.

Toe-guard Bracket mounted to the swingarm which protects the rider's foot from contacting the chain or rear sprocket in the event of a crash. Sometimes called a Shark fin.

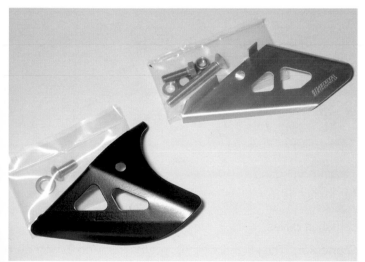

Torque Turning or twisting force about a shaft.

Torque setting A prescribed tightness specified by the motorcycle manufacturer to ensure that the bolt or nut is secured correctly. Undertightening can result in the bolt or nut coming loose or a surface not being sealed. Overtightening can result in stripped threads, distortion or damage to the component being retained.

Torx key A six-point wrench.

Tracer A stripe of a second colour applied to a wire insulator to distinguish that wire from another one with the same colour insulator. For example, Br/W is often used to denote a brown insulator with a white tracer.

Track day Regular events organised by race tracks for riding under race conditions.

Trail A feature of steering geometry. Distance from the steering head axis to the tyre's central contact point.

Turbocharger A centrifugal device, driven by exhaust gases, that pressurises the intake air. Normally used to increase the power output from a given engine displacement.

TWI Abbreviation for Tyre Wear Indicator. Indicates the location of the tread depth indicator bars on tyres.

Undertray Plastic or fibreglass panel which fits in place of the rear mudguard, usually colour coded to the bikes paintwork.

Unsprung weight Anything not supported by the bike's suspension (e.g. the wheel, tyres, brakes, final drive and bottom (moving) part of the suspension).

Vacuum gauges Clock-type gauges for measuring intake tract vacuum. Used for carburettor synchronisation. A manometer is also used for the same purpose.

Valve A device through which the flow of liquid, gas or vacuum may be stopped, started or regulated by a moveable part that opens, shuts or partially obstructs one or more ports or passageways. The intake and exhaust valves in the cylinder head are of the poppet type.

Valve clearance The clearance between the valve tip (the end of the valve stem) and the rocker arm or tappet/follower. The valve clearance is measured when the valve is closed. The correct clearance is important – if too small the valve won't close fully and will burn out, whereas if too large noisy operation will result.

Valve lift The amount a valve is lifted off its seat by the camshaft lobe.

Valve timing The exact setting for the opening and closing of the valves in relation to piston position.

VIN Vehicle Identification Number. Term for the bike's engine and frame numbers.

Viscosity The thickness of a liquid or its resistance to flow.

Volt A unit for expressing electrical "pressure" in a circuit. Volts = current x ohms.

Watt A unit for expressing electrical power. Watts = volts x current.

Wheelbase Distance from the centre of the front wheel to the centre of the rear wheel.

Wiring harness or loom Describes the electrical wires running the length of the motorcycle and enclosed in tape or plastic sheathing. Wiring coming off the main harness is usually referred to as a sub-harness.

Index

A

Air filters 40
Alarms 14
Allen keys and bits 132
Aspect ratio (tyre) 90

B

Bar end protectors 124
Bar grips 72
Bars and controls 70
Bike/frame protectors 125
Bodypanels 109
Bodywork 94
    bolt kits 116
    carbon fibre 105
    decals 114
    fuel caps 98
    repair 111
    screens 94
    tank pads 97
    undertrays 100
Bolt kits 116
Braided hoses 66
Brake lever lock 14
Brakes 60
    discs 62-65
    fluid 62
    hoses 66
    light switch 78
    master cylinder 68
    pads 61
Breaker bar 131

C

C-spanner 133
Carbon fibre 105, 129
Chain 82-86
Chain (security) 12
Chain care 86
Chain and sprockets 80
Chainguards 87
Clear lenses 16, 17
Clip-ons 71
Clutches 34
Compression damping 50
Crash protectors 123
Crimping pliers 133

D

Decals 114
Dial kits 25
Digital gear indicator 25-29
Disc lock 13
Discs 62-65
Dynamometer 43
Dyno-jet kit 42

E

Engine casings 128
Engine management display 30
Exhaust cleaning and baffles 40
Exhaust fitting 36-39
Exhaust protectors 124
Exhaust repacking 36
Exhaust systems 35

F

Filter (air) 40
Flush-mounted indicators 19
Frame guards 108
Front fork
    adjustment 47-52
    protectors 126
    upgrades 54
    travel 51
Front mudguard 107, 110
Front sprocket 80
Front sprocket cover 108
Fuel caps 98
Fuel system control 42

G

Gear indicator 25-29
Gear ratio 86
Ground anchor 15

H

Headlight bulbs 21
Headlight covers 22
Heel guards 79
HT leads 33
Hugger 106, 110

I

Ignition coils 33
Indicators 17, 18
Iridium plugs 33

J

Jack-up plates 79

L

LEDs 20, 100
Licence plate 104
Lighting and mirrors 16
Load index (tyre) 90
Locks 12

M

Master cylinder (radial)
    clutch 34
    front brake 68
Mini indicators 18
Mirrors 23
Mudguard 107, 110

P

Pads (brake) 61
Performance 32
Plastic bodywork repair 111
Plugs and leads 33
Power Commander 44
Pre-load adjustment 47

R

Race bodywork 109
Radial master cylinder 34, 68
Rainbow strobes 21
Rear hugger 106, 110
Rear sets 73-77
Rear shock
    adjustment 47-52
    upgrade 52
Rear sprocket 81
Rebound damping 52
Replica replacement bodywork 109
Rev light 30
Re-valving front forks 55
Rim sizes 90

S

Safety 10
Screens 94
Screwdrivers 131
Security 12
Security bolts and marking kits 14
Shift light 30
Single seat unit 110
Slipper clutch 34
Socket sets 132
Spanners 131
Spark plugs and leads 33
Speed symbol/rating (tyre) 90
Spring sag and pre-load 47
Springs (front fork) 54
Sprockets 80
Steering dampers 56
Suspension adjustment 47
Suspension and Steering 46
Swingarm 55
Swingarm protectors 123

T

Tail light 16, 100
Tail tidy 104
Tank pads 97
Toe guards 127
Tools 131
Torque wrench 132
Track days 118
    bodywork 109
Tyres 88

U

U-lock 13
Undertrays 100

V

Visual displays 24

W

Well-nuts 95
Wheel clamp 15
Wheel rim decals/transfers 92
Wheels 91
    alignment 87
Wire cutters 133

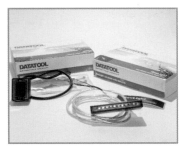

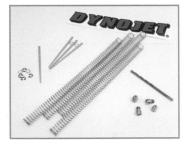

Thanks to:

We gratefully acknowledge all the help and advice given by the following manufacturers, suppliers and dealers.

Acumen Electronics Ltd
01264 359922
www.acumen-electronics.co.uk

Bike Torque Racing
01373 464252
www.biketorqueracing.co.uk

Bransons Motorcycles
01935 474998
www.bransonsmotorcycles.co.uk

Castle Combe Race Track
01249 782417
www.castlecombecircuit.co.uk

Cooper-Avon Tyres Ltd
01225 703101
www.avonmotorcycle.com

Crescent Suzuki Verwood
01202 820170
www.crescent-suzuki.com

Data Tool (UK) Ltd
0870 165 2414
www.datatool.co.uk

Demon Tweeks
01978 664474
www.demon-tweeks.co.uk

Dynojet UK Ltd
01995 600500
www.dynojet.co.uk

EBC Brakes
01604 583344
www.ebcbrakes.com

Harris Performance Products Ltd
01992 532500
www.harris-performance.com

HEL Performance Products
01392 811601
www.helperformance.com

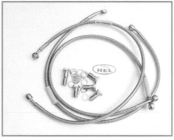

Performance Parts Ltd
0870 240 2118
www.performanceparts-ltd.com

Pro Bolt Ltd
01684 851940
www.tastynuts.com

R & G Racing Products
01420 521100
www.rg-racing.com

Skidmarx UK Ltd
01305 780808
www.skidmarx.co.uk

Talon Engineering Ltd
01935 471508
www.talon-eng.co.uk

Yeovil Motorcycles
01935 415815
www.yeovilmotorcycles.com

A special thank you to:
Adam Jordan (technical advice)
Andy 'Aprilia' Swindells

Workshop
Pete Gill

Photography
Emmeline Wilmott

Design and page build
James Robertson

Editor
Penny Cox

Production control
Charles Seaton

Haynes Motorcycle Manuals – The Complete List

Title	Book No
APRILIA RSV1000 Mille (98 - 03)	4255
BMW 2-valve Twins (70 - 96)	♦ 0249
BMW K100 & 75 2-valve Models (83 - 96)	♦ 1373
BMW R850, 1100 & 1150 4-valve Twins (93 - 04)	♦ 3466
BSA Bantam (48 - 71)	0117
BSA Unit Singles (58 - 72)	0127
BSA Pre-unit Singles (54 - 61)	0326
BSA A7 & A10 Twins (47 - 62)	0121
BSA A50 & A65 Twins (62 - 73)	0155
DUCATI 600, 750 & 900 2-valve V-Twins (91 - 96)	♦ 3290
Ducati MK III & Desmo Singles (69 - 76)	◇ 0445
Ducati 748, 916 & 996 4-valve V-Twins (94 - 01)	♦ 3756
GILERA Runner, DNA, Stalker & Ice (97 - 04)	4163
HARLEY-DAVIDSON Sportsters (70 - 03)	♦ 2534
Harley-Davidson Shovelhead and Evolution Big Twins (70 - 99)	2536
Harley-Davidson Twin Cam 88 (99 - 03)	♦ 2478
HONDA NB, ND, NP & NS50 Melody (81 - 85)	◇ 0622
Honda NE/NB50 Vision & SA50 Vision Met-in (85 - 95)	◇ 1278
Honda MB, MBX, MT & MTX50 (80 - 93)	0731
Honda C50, C70 & C90 (67 - 99)	0324
Honda XR80R & XR100R (85 - 04)	2218
Honda XL/XR 80, 100, 125, 185 & 200 2-valve Models (78 - 87)	0566
Honda H100 & H100S Singles (80 - 92)	◇ 0734
Honda CB/CD125T & CM125C Twins (77 - 88)	◇ 0571
Honda CG125 (76 - 00)	◇ 0433
Honda NS125 (86 - 93)	3056
Honda MBX/MTX125 & MTX200 (83 - 93)	◇ 1132
Honda CD/CM185 200T & CM250C 2-valve Twins (77 - 85)	0572
Honda XL/XR 250 & 500 (78 - 84)	0567
Honda XR250L, XR250R & XR400R (86 - 03)	2219
Honda CB250 & CB400N Super Dreams (78 - 84)	◇ 0540
Honda CR Motocross Bikes (86 - 01)	2222
Honda CBR400RR Fours (88 - 99)	◇ ♦ 3552
Honda VFR400 (NC30) & RVF400 (NC35) V-Fours (89 - 98)	◇ ♦ 3496
Honda CB500 (93 - 01)	◇ ♦ 3753
Honda CB400 & CB550 Fours (73 - 77)	0262
Honda CX/GL500 & 650 V-Twins (78 - 86)	0442
Honda CBX550 Four (82 - 86)	◇ 0940
Honda XL600R & XR600R (83 - 00)	2183
Honda XL600/650V Transalp & XRV750 Africa Twin (87 - 02)	◇ 3919
Honda CBR600F1 & 1000F Fours (87 - 96)	♦ 1730
Honda CBR600F2 & F3 Fours (91 - 98)	♦ 2070
Honda CBR600F4 (99 - 02)	♦ 3911
Honda CB600F Hornet (98 - 02)	◇ ♦ 3915
Honda CB650 sohc Fours (78 - 84)	0665
Honda NTV600 Revere, NTV650 & NT650V Deauville (88 - 01)	◇ 3243
Honda Shadow VT600 & 750 (USA) (88 - 03)	2312
Honda CB750 sohc Four (69 - 79)	0131
Honda V45/65 Sabre & Magna (82 - 88)	0820
Honda VFR750 & 700 V-Fours (86 - 97)	♦ 2101
Honda VFR800 V-Fours (97 - 01)	♦ 3703
Honda VFR800 V-Tec V-Fours (02 - 05)	♦ 4196
Honda CB750 & CB900 dohc Fours (78 - 84)	0535
Honda VTR1000 (FireStorm, Super Hawk) & XL1000V (Varadero) (97 - 00)	♦ 3744
Honda CBR900RR FireBlade (92 - 99)	♦ 2161
Honda CBR900RR FireBlade (00 - 03)	♦ 4060
Honda CBR1100XX Super Blackbird (97 - 02)	♦ 3901
Honda ST1100 Pan European V-Fours (90 - 01)	♦ 3384
Honda Shadow VT1100 (USA) (85 - 98)	2313

Title	Book No
Honda GL1000 Gold Wing (75 - 79)	0309
Honda GL1100 Gold Wing (79 - 81)	0669
Honda Gold Wing 1200 (USA) (84 - 87)	2199
Honda Gold Wing 1500 (USA) (88 - 00)	2225
KAWASAKI AE/AR 50 & 80 (81 - 95)	1007
Kawasaki KC, KE & KH100 (75 - 99)	1371
Kawasaki KMX125 & 200 (86 - 02)	◇ 3046
Kawasaki 250, 350 & 400 Triples (72 - 79)	0134
Kawasaki 400 & 440 Twins (74 - 81)	0281
Kawasaki 400, 500 & 550 Fours (79 - 91)	0910
Kawasaki EN450 & 500 Twins (Ltd/Vulcan) (85 - 04)	2053
Kawasaki EX & ER500 (GPZ500S & ER-5) Twins (87 - 99)	♦ 2052
Kawasaki ZX600 (Ninja ZX-6, ZZ-R600) Fours (90 - 00)	♦ 2146
Kawasaki ZX-6R Ninja Fours (95 - 02)	♦ 3541
Kawasaki ZX600 (GPZ600R, GPX600R, Ninja 600R & RX) & ZX750 (GPX750R, Ninja 750R) Fours (85 - 97)	♦ 1780
Kawasaki 650 Four (76 - 78)	0373
Kawasaki Vulcan 700/750 & 800 (85 - 04)	♦ 2457
Kawasaki 750 Air-cooled Fours (80 - 91)	0574
Kawasaki ZR550 & 750 Zephyr Fours (90 - 97)	♦ 3382
Kawasaki ZX750 (Ninja ZX-7 & ZXR750) Fours (89 - 96)	♦ 2054
Kawasaki Ninja ZX-7R & ZX-9R (94 - 04)	♦ 3721
Kawasaki 900 & 1000 Fours (73 - 77)	0222
Kawasaki ZX900, 1000 & 1100 Liquid-cooled Fours (83 - 97)	♦ 1681
MOTO GUZZI 750, 850 & 1000 V-Twins (74 - 78)	0339
MZ ETZ Models (81 - 95)	◇ 1680
NORTON 500, 600, 650 & 750 Twins (57 - 70)	0187
Norton Commando (68 - 77)	0125
PEUGEOT Speedfight, Trekker & Vivacity (96 - 02)	◇ 3920
PIAGGIO (Vespa) Scooters (91 - 03)	◇ 3492
SUZUKI GT, ZR & TS50 (77 - 90)	◇ 0799
Suzuki TS50X (84 - 00)	◇ 1599
Suzuki 100, 125, 185 & 250 Air-cooled Trail bikes (79 - 89)	0797
Suzuki GP100 & 125 Singles (78 - 93)	◇ 0576
Suzuki GS, GN, GZ & DR125 Singles (82 - 99)	◇ 0888
Suzuki 250 & 350 Twins (68 - 78)	0120
Suzuki GT250X7, GT200X5 & SB200 Twins (78 - 83)	◇ 0469
Suzuki GS/GSX250, 400 & 450 Twins (79 - 85)	0736
Suzuki GS500 Twin (89 - 02)	♦ 3238
Suzuki GS550 (77 - 82) & GS750 Fours (76 - 79)	0363
Suzuki GS/GSX550 4-valve Fours (83 - 88)	1133
Suzuki SV650 (99 - 02)	♦ 3912
Suzuki GSX-R600 & 750 (96 - 00)	♦ 3553
Suzuki GSX-R600 (01 - 02), GSX-R750 (00 - 02) & GSX-R1000 (01 - 02)	♦ 3986
Suzuki GSF600 & 1200 Bandit Fours (95 - 04)	♦ 3367
Suzuki GS850 Fours (78 - 88)	0536
Suzuki GS1000 Four (77 - 79)	0484
Suzuki GSX-R750, GSX-R1100 (85 - 92), GSX600F, GSX750F, GSX1100F (Katana) Fours (88 - 96)	♦ 2055
Suzuki GSX600/750F & GSX750 (98 - 02)	♦ 3987
Suzuki GS/GSX1000, 1100 & 1150 4-valve Fours (79 - 88)	0737
Suzuki TL1000S/R & DL1000 V-Strom (97 - 04)	♦ 4083
Suzuki GSX1300R Hayabusa (99 - 04)	♦ 4184
TRIUMPH Tiger Cub & Terrier (52 - 68)	0414
Triumph 350 & 500 Unit Twins (58 - 73)	0137
Triumph Pre-Unit Twins (47 - 62)	0251
Triumph 650 & 750 2-valve Unit Twins (63 - 83)	0122
Triumph Trident & BSA Rocket 3 (69 - 75)	0136
Triumph Fuel Injected Triples (97 - 00)	♦ 3755
Triumph Triples & Fours (carburettor engines) (91 - 99)	♦ 2162
VESPA P/PX125, 150 & 200 Scooters (78 - 03)	0707
Vespa Scooters (59 - 78)	0126
YAMAHA DT50 & 80 Trail Bikes (78 - 95)	◇ 0800

Title	Book No
Yamaha T50 & 80 Townmate (83 - 95)	◇ 1247
Yamaha YB100 Singles (73 - 91)	◇ 0474
Yamaha RS/RXS100 & 125 Singles (74 - 95)	0331
Yamaha RD & DT125LC (82 - 87)	◇ 0887
Yamaha TZR125 (87 - 93) & DT125R (88 - 02)	◇ 1655
Yamaha TY50, 80, 125 & 175 (74 - 84)	◇ 0464
Yamaha XT & SR125 (82 - 02)	◇ 1021
Yamaha Trail Bikes (81 - 00)	2350
Yamaha 250 & 350 Twins (70 - 79)	0040
Yamaha XS250, 360 & 400 sohc Twins (75 - 84)	0378
Yamaha RD250 & 350LC Twins (80 - 82)	0803
Yamaha RD350 YPVS Twins (83 - 95)	1158
Yamaha RD400 Twin (75 - 79)	0333
Yamaha XT, TT & SR500 Singles (75 - 83)	0342
Yamaha XZ550 Vision V-Twins (82 - 85)	0821
Yamaha FJ, FZ, XJ & YX600 Radian (84 - 92)	2100
Yamaha XJ600S (Diversion, Seca II) & XJ600N Fours (92 - 03)	♦ 2145
Yamaha YZF600R Thundercat & FZS600 Fazer (96 - 03)	♦ 3702
Yamaha YZF-R6 (98 - 02)	♦ 3900
Yamaha 650 Twins (70 - 83)	0341
Yamaha XJ650 & 750 Fours (80 - 84)	0738
Yamaha XS750 & 850 Triples (76 - 85)	0340
Yamaha TDM850, TRX850 & XTZ750 (89 - 99)	◇ ♦ 3540
Yamaha YZF750R & YZF1000R Thunderace (93 - 00)	♦ 3720
Yamaha FZR600, 750 & 1000 Fours (87 - 96)	♦ 2056
Yamaha XV (Virago) V-Twins (81 - 03)	♦ 0802
Yamaha XVS650 & 1100 Dragstar/V-Star (97 - 05)	♦ 4195
Yamaha XJ900F Fours (83 - 94)	♦ 3239
Yamaha XJ900S Diversion (94 - 01)	♦ 3739
Yamaha YZF-R1 (98 - 03)	♦ 3754
Yamaha FJ1100 & 1200 Fours (84 - 96)	♦ 2057
Yamaha XJR1200 & 1300 (95 - 03)	♦ 3981
Yamaha V-Max (85 - 03)	♦ 4072
ATVs	
Honda ATC70, 90, 110, 185 & 200 (71 - 85)	0565
Honda TRX300 Shaft Drive ATVs (88 - 00)	2125
Honda TRX300EX & TRX400EX ATVs (93 - 04)	2318
Honda Foreman 400 and 450 ATVs (95 - 02)	2465
Kawasaki Bayou 220/250/300 & Prairie 300 ATVs (86 - 03)	2351
Polaris ATVs (85 - 97)	2302
Polaris ATVs (98 - 03)	2508
Yamaha YFS200 Blaster ATV (88 - 02)	2317
Yamaha YFB250 Timberwolf ATVs (92 - 00)	2217
Yamaha YFM350 & YFM400 (ER and Big Bear) ATVs (87 - 03)	2126
Yamaha Banshee and Warrior ATVs (87 - 03)	2314
ATV Basics	10450
TECHBOOK SERIES	
Motorcycle Basics TechBook (2nd Edition)	3515
Motorcycle Electrical TechBook (3rd Edition)	3471
Motorcycle Fuel Systems TechBook	3514
Motorcycle Maintenance TechBook	4071
Motorcycle Workshop Practice TechBook (2nd Edition)	3470
GENERAL MANUALS	
Twist and Go (automatic transmission) Scooters Service and Repair Manual	4082

◇ = not available in the USA   ♦ = Superbike

The manuals on this page are available through good motorcycle dealers and accessory shops.
In case of difficulty, contact: **Haynes Publishing**
(UK) +44 1963 442030   (USA) +1 805 498 6703
(FR) +33 1 47 17 66 29   (SV) +46 18 124016
(Australia/New Zealand) +61 3 9763 8100